As the feet of a trained dancer, my Raevyn established the necessary muscle to adjust to the rhythm of her life. Having mastered the *first position* of early childhood, Rae, as I affectionately call her, began this journey she writes about with great fervor and tenacity. *Second position* finds her developing the additional skills she'll need to pen the swift transitions of her times. *Third position's* step forward preps her for the intricate Master's choreography. The sometimes dramatic twist and turns of her relationship with God and others, twirls this young writer to reflect and journal what would become the very happenings of these pages. *Fourth position* finds her balanced and poised, having leaped over hurdles, sashayed through tough places, prepared to be lunged forward, toward her divine, ordained destiny, as we experience why ***Raevyn was made.***

Mommy

WHAT ALMOST KILLED ME
MADE ME

WHAT ALMOST KILLED ME
MADE ME

RAEVYN

authorHOUSE®

AuthorHouse™ LLC
1663 Liberty Drive
Bloomington, IN 47403
www.authorhouse.com
Phone: 1-800-839-8640

Cover Design: Dae Enterprise
Hair and Make Up: Temolynn Wintons
Styling: Raevyn

Published by AuthorHouse 04/01/2014

ISBN: 978-1-4918-5157-9 (sc)
ISBN: 978-1-4918-5156-2 (hc)
ISBN: 978-1-4918-5158-6 (e)

Library of Congress Control Number: 2014900804

DEDICATION

This book is dedicated to every ex-boyfriend, so-called friend, trifling father, liar, cheater, manipulator, gossiper and hater. If it were not for you and your selfish motivation, I would not have been propelled to share MY story. Thank you for igniting me to pursue and execute my passion, to walk in my God-given calling, and to strive to become the best version of myself possible. Your lies and words of discouragement fueled me to be all that you said I was, was not, and more.

Haters are HELP, and I was taught not to argue with the help.

Thank you

PREFACE

What Almost Killed Me MADE ME is comprised of my thoughts, life experiences, and lessons learned. Even though they are all depicted in the form of written word they are a romance-drama movie, my favorite song that plays on repeat, a scripted reality show DVR'd, Facebook statuses liked, tweets re-tweeted, and all the many poems, spoken-word lyrics, love and hate letters that were never exposed, yet inspired and provoked by the best professor ever known to man: Life.

Names have been changed to protect the guilty. ;)

CONTENTS

INTRODUCTION

Everyone has a story. Each phase in life is just another chapter. Some are more entertaining than others, but they all play a vital part in the end. As a form of therapy and ministry, I chronicled the first quarter of my life. This memoir is my story thus far.

Reality television is the new phenomenon of people living their lives in the public eye. I never really understood why someone would allow cameras to document some of the most personal moments in one's life. I will admit, I am guilty of indulging in some of these shows and found myself invested, involved and entertained by someone else's life story, wasting my time watching their life as my own reality was passing me by.

So I decided to take back control of my reality and share my story with the world. Not to slander myself, but in hopes of helping someone. I have chosen to willingly offer my life as a vessel to be used by God. Yes, I may be embarrassed by my poor choices. Yes, I may have fear that people will look at me differently when they know my story. But this is my life. My ministry. I refuse to allow the devil to win and keep me quiet and bound. The only way to be free is to expose the blackmailer, which is the devil.

The episodes and chapters of my life are not for monetary gain or entertainment purposes, but to hopefully reach that one young girl who has had a few bad chapters in her life and at the point of nearing her conclusion prematurely. If the growing pains of my life is for that one girl, then all the pain and disappointment was worth it.

As I write this memoir, I keep trying to force the words, sentences and chapters to flow. I didn't want the reader to be confused or mixed up. I wanted my writing to be perfect. But the more I tried to make this book grammatically and politically correct, the more it wasn't. As I wrote and rewrote the same sentence over and over, I realized that this is my life's story. Life doesn't flow. It's not grammatically or politically correct. And it's definitely not perfect. It's life. It's not an easy read. It is confusing and mixed up at times. There may be run-on sentences, incorrect punctuations, misspelled words, a little ebonics, and some entirely too long chapters. But when I reflect back, that was my life. As much as I tried to rewrite the sentences and chapters of my life to make it a perfect body of work, it still turned out to be filled with flaws, typos, incorrect verb tenses, and unedited chapters. So be prepared to go on this journey with me. Hopefully you are able to follow along as I share my heart, my testimony, my story, and my life in its most raw and realest form.

CHAPTER

WHAT THE DEVIL
MEANT FOR BAD . . .

God will ALWAYS turn it
around for His good

 The time came for a 24-year-old woman to go into labor. Contractions came minute after minute. The woman was screaming and pushing; the doctor informed her that the child was breech. During labor, the baby pushed, fought and forced its way out sideways. The doctors were troubled and did not believe that the mother or the child would live. The doctor gave the woman's parents a difficult decision to make—whether to save the life of their daughter or their unborn grandchild. The parents prayed and told the doctor that they would like for him to save both of them, but if they had to choose they wanted him to save their daughter. Their reasoning was they had a relationship with their daughter but did not know their unborn grandchild. Hopefully, their daughter would be able to conceive and birth another child. The mother, however, refused to make that choice and was willing and determined to risk her life to save her child's life. She pressed through the pain and fought hard until she birthed a healthy baby girl. That baby girl was me, Raevyn Trai-Joie White Jefferson. Who would have thought that I had to fight my way into this world and would have to continue fighting once I arrived?

The devil intended to take my mother and me out because he knew we'd be a force to be reckoned with. What he didn't know was he added to our artillery. Now my mom is able to discern and minister to women who are abused verbally, emotionally and physically. She is able to use what was supposed to be her life-ending story, to breathe new life into the women who are in unhealthy relationships, or allow the secrets they have chosen to take to the grave, not to drive them to their grave. That ol' devil's plan backfired. Through tragedy, pain and fear God prevailed. My mom and I are still fighting for our lives and we refuse to choose to die. He didn't know that the same strength and determination I had to use as a newborn to fight my way into this world is the same drive I would use to get me through my life's battles. He messed with the wrong two people, and with every part of my being I will fulfill the great calling on my life. That child that the devil didn't want to come into this world is going to take this world by storm for the Kingdom of God!

Having to live through experiencing a life threatening pregnancy and almost losing your unborn child could have taken my mom out. But God! Just take a moment to think about all of the pain and tragedies in your life that could have taken you out, made you give up or die. Then, take a second and think about the promise and purpose that came of those times. Some tragedies may not have been God-sent, but they will definitely be God used. God may not send certain situations in our lives, but He has a way of using it ALL for His glory. Rest assured, God will get His glory through your story.

Raevyn

HOME

My mom wrote and directed a stage play entitled "Home" adapted from both the Broadway musical *The Wiz* as well as the classic film *The Wizard of Oz*. My character was the leading role of Purity, similar to Dorothy in *The Wiz*. The play tells the journey of a young girl striving to find her way home. However, unlike Dorothy, Purity does not find her home in Kansas. She finds her home in the church within the grace of God.

Purity goes through an exciting, yet life changing spiritual journey in which she fights off various sins and temptations, wins over lost souls to Christ and finds her true "home" with the Lord back in church.

The Angel of Light played by my aunt helps to narrate the play and plays an active role in attempting to protect Purity throughout her journey. She delivers the Armourbearer to help Purity in her time of need. The Armourbearer provides Purity and her friends with the sword of the spirit, the shield of faith, the breastplate of righteousness, and the helmet of salvation to assist in their battle against evil.

The angel of light also provides Purity with a host of spiritual virtues also known as the fruit of the spirit: love, joy, peace, longsuffering, kindness, goodness, faithfulness, gentleness and temperance. However, the angel of darkness also narrates the play and takes an active role in attempting to lead Purity astray from the light of God and into darkness and despair. The angel of darkness delivers Demonica to divert the attention of Purity from God. Demonica unleashes the weeds of the spirit upon Purity and her friends. The weeds included sorrow, confusion, impatience, meanness, badness, unreliableness, harshness and out of control, all direct opposites of the fruit of the spirit.

Purity's journey begins in a jubilant church service. The preacher begins with a powerful message to the choir and congregation. As the choir sings and congregation worship, Purity slumbers off to sleep next to her mother and begins to dream.

Just as the Scarecrow, Lion and Tin Man became the main sources of strength for Dorothy in the *Wizard of Oz*, the preacher, the usher and the deacon served as the three main allies to Purity in *Home*, however these three characters take on different forms in the dreams of Purity. They become a pimp, drug user, and drug dealer.

The character Angie Girlfriend encourages Purity in the garden of the fruit of the spirit to remain on the straight and narrow path.

Then, the real trials and tribulations begin. Purity journeys to the wrong part of town. She wards off the temptations offered by the pimp, drug user and drug dealer and invites each of them to Christ. Purity prays her way, presses her way and praises her way on home.

During the journey, good confronts evil initiating physical and spiritual warfare. After an arduous battle, light triumphs over darkness. However, the victory only proves to be temporary, for the angel of darkness still has tricks up her sleeve, an all-out war ensues between good and evil. The angel of light provides Purity and her friends with the spiritual guidance and preparation from the angel of the North. After receiving spiritual impartation and covering, Purity finds her way back Home.

Lesson Learned:

Purity was not just a character; she portrayed me on a spiritual journey striving to find my way home. Home represented my rightful place in God, my purpose, my safety, and one day heaven. Purity faced many trials, setbacks, distractions and demons that wanted to steal her praise, but she reverted to what she knew would help her. She pleaded the blood of Jesus.

There are so many times when I have found myself in "weedsville" being attacked by the enemy, and all I know to do cry out the name of Jesus and he has no choice but to flee. When your journey becomes hard and you need to find your way home always know that you have the angel of light, Angie Girlfriend, the fruit of the Spirit and the angel of the North on the journey with you. You are never alone. You have enough to go on. Just follow the Spirit as you pray your way, press your way, and praise your way on home.

LOVE CENTER MINISTRIES
of Apalachicola, FL

presents

"HOME"

an evangelistic gospel musical play,
inspired by and adapted from the broadway
musical "The Wiz" and the move "The Wonderful
Wizard of Oz"

written and directed by
Temolynne White Wintons

an LCCI Production

NOTES

CHAPTER

ENGAGED
BUT
NOT MARRIED

"If you want to make God
laugh, tell Him your plans."

Anyone that knows me will tell you that I am a hopeful—not hopeless—romantic and a huge sucker for love. Ever since I was little, I always had the desire to marry young and for my husband and me to be this kingdom couple. I wanted us to minister to other young couples and young people about being souled out for Christ. Ever since I could remember, I always wanted to do the right thing by God. My heart has always been pure before Him, and I always have wanted to please Him.

I knew my weaknesses, and lust was definitely one of them, so I wanted to beat the devil running by getting married young and avoiding sexual sin. The harder I pushed to be married, though, the more disappointment and hurt I brought to myself. My best friend always called me the motherly, wifey type because I enjoyed cooking (a good cook I might add), grocery shopping, cleaning, home decorating, etc.—all of the stuff she considered someone who had a husband and family should be doing, not a 21-year-old college student with no husband or family. I would always laugh when she made those comments, but that was a part of who I am, a nurturer. She also would say that these guys were stupid "not to wife you up" because "you are the total package—you cook, clean, smart, educated and a godly woman." She believed that there were not many young women around these days that did any of these things and definitely not all of them.

However, that was my hang up. I would date a guy and treat him as if he were my husband already. I did not put up a front to act like I was something that I was not, I just was giving him too many of the benefits without him having any of the responsibility.

Lesson Learned: If you are dating a guy, and he has not put a ring on it, then he does not deserve hubby benefits. It is not smart to invest your time, finances and body into someone who can easily get up and walk away without any papers being signed. Oh let me tell you, this one guy I dated I registered him for college, filled out financial aid paperwork, helped or did his homework, met with advisors, helped to pay his bills, bought groceries, cooked breakfast, lunch and dinner and more things that I am too embarrassed to name. I did not realize then that I was investing too much of myself into this man that was not my husband. This negro could easily decide to up and leave me and let the next chick reap all of *my* benefits that I worked so hard for. Which is what happened (read The Relationship from Hell chapter). After a few failed engagements, I have come to realize that it takes a true God-fearing man to commit to God and me in holy matrimony. Many have asked, "Will you marry me," but no one could man up and say, "I do."

You would think that God would grant me my desire to be married since marriage is biblical and God honors marriage, right? Well, I have come to realize two-and-a-half engagements later that my so called fairy tale relationship and marriage that I thought I wanted was not what God had planned for my life at that time and with those men. Like the saying goes, "If you want to make God laugh, tell Him your plans." If I knew then what I know now, a lot of pain, hurt, disappointments and tears could have been avoided. However, then I would not be writing this book because I would not have gone through anything to write about. So I know that it all had a purpose.

Raevyn

A BROKEN ENGAGEMENT IS BETTER THAN A BROKEN MARRIAGE

Yes, I have been engaged 2.5 times, and I am not ashamed or embarrassed to admit that. When I was going through pre-marital counseling with my second fiancée, the best advice I received was "A broken engagement is better than a broken marriage." When the pastor said that, it resonated with me and released me to make decisions for the good of me—not my fiancée, our families or friends, but for me. There are too many marriages that were already over before they started. Once wedding preparations are underway, couples feel trapped and don't want to disappoint their love ones. I would rather have love ones temporarily disappointed rather than a lifetime of unhappiness. My counselor said if I was walking down the aisle on my wedding day and felt deep down in my heart like this was not what I wanted to do, it would be best to call it off then and tell our guests that the reception is already paid for and feel free to enjoy themselves, however, the wedding ceremony will not be taking place. That sounds crazy, but sometimes it is for the best. Don't set yourself up for failure and expect things to change once you are married. It doesn't work that way.

One of the reasons why divorce rates are so high is because couples knew they were not ready for the marriage but went through with the wedding anyway. When in doubt, communicate with your partner and ask God for guidance and direction. There is nothing wrong with having a failed engagement. At least you had the strength to deal with the problem and make the best choice for you and ultimately the other person in the long run.

14

My first engagement ended mutually. We were high school sweethearts; Ray was my first love and my first sexual partner. He was older, raised in the streets and a thug, but he was my best friend. Yes, we were in love and wanted to do the right thing by God, but we outgrew each other and were at two different places in life. I was going off to college, and he didn't know where his life was going.

Ray was murdered a year or so after we decided not to get married. God always knows what is best for us. We just have to trust Him, even when we have no clue what lies ahead. Trust your heart and spirit and know that God will not lead you astray.

My second engagement I called off because I just knew that he was not the one for me and I was not the one for him. He was a great guy, an excellent boyfriend and fiancée, and would make someone a wonderful husband, just not me. I cared about him enough that I did not want to ruin his life by marrying him. Making the decision to hurt him and let him go was difficult, but that temporary pain was worth it knowing that I made the best decision for the both of us. I always wanted him to find someone that loved him as much as he loved me. Thankfully, a year later he was engaged and eventually married. I have not spoken to him since we went our separate ways, but I feel peace knowing that he has moved on and has happily married.

Lessons Learned: Just because something is right does not mean that it is right for you or the right time for you. Don't give up! Look up! Ask God for His guidance, He will give you His perfect will for your life. Do not give someone a position in your life (i.e. husband) that they are not qualified for and have not been sworn in to accept. Just pray for God to give you the person you are supposed to have in the season you are supposed to have them.

KNOW YOUR SELF WORTH

Jesus Christ loved us so much that He gave His life for you and me. If someone would sacrifice their life for our sins so that we may live, we must be worth a lot. So why is it that we devalue ourselves? Why do we allow men and women to treat us as if we are worthless? One day I had an ah-ha moment when I realized my value. When I fell in love with myself and appraised just how much I am worth, I refused to ever settle for less than I deserved again. I am not only speaking of material value, but how I should be treated and the level of respect I should receive at all times. As black women, we already have a negative connotation of being nagging, complaining, always having an attitude, etc. I beg to differ, it's not that we have an attitude or we complain about what men are not doing, we just won't settle for having an half *** man treat us any kind of way. You date and marry at the level of your self-esteem. If you are insecure, not confident and your value is depreciating then that is the type of person you will end up with. If you know that you are precious, rare and worth the best, then that is exactly the kind of person you will be with, and they will treat you accordingly.

NOTES

_____

_____

_____

_____

_____

_____

_____

_____

_____

CHAPTER

3

THAT'S ALL YOU GOT?

I may have done what you said I did,
but I am not who you say I am.

One morning during training at my new job, I get a voicemail from one of my closest friends. The voicemail says that it wasn't an emergency but to call her back. I give her a call, and she begins to tell me that my juvenile record has been exposed. She tells me that somebody in my hometown or surrounding area that works for a correctional facility has ran a background check on me and has showed my record to everybody. I guess she was waiting on a reaction from me, however, I just continued to listen. I asked her who told her and she said that her boyfriend, who works for the Department of Corrections, told her that somebody showed him. Supposedly the "hot news" was all over the panhandle of Florida. After I listened to her without interruption, all I had to say was "I must be doing something right because that's when people start talking about you."

When I hung up the phone, I was not disturbed or bothered at all. I thought back to a message I had just heard at church. The title of his message was "I Feel Something Coming." The preacher said, "When people stop talking about you, you are losing your edge." We need at least one real enemy who is going to stay on assignment at all times. So when I thought back to that message, all I could say was, "Is that all you got devil? Is that really the best you can do?" The devil was so five years ago. The word on the street was true. It was not a rumor. However, nobody really knew the whole story or the truth. I did have a criminal record; I was arrested three times for the same thing.

Back in college I was so spoiled and accustomed to having everything I wanted, that when I didn't have the money to get what I wanted, I was determined to get it by any means necessary, even if it meant stealing. I would go into department stores and buy one or two items and steal five items in my purse. You would think after getting caught the first time I would have learned my lesson, but the devil can have you so blinded and messed up your head that you think you are smarter than you really are and won't get caught again. Yeah right! So the first time I got caught, since it was my first time ever being in trouble, I was released on ROR and given the diversion program, which meant that as long as I paid the fees, completed my community service, and attended a class, the charge would be dropped and erased from my record. I completed the program and never told anyone about it.

You would think that I would have learned my lesson and thanked God for not allowing this situation to be exposed. Nope! Not "invincible, I can get away with anything Raevyn". Less than a month later I did the same exact thing (at a different store at least) all over again. I got caught (of course), but I didn't have to go to jail, though I had to appear in court. The judge gave me adjudication withheld and probation. Who would have ever thought that Raevyn Jefferson was on probation? I'm sure even if I told people that they would have believed me. I completed my probation early, sealed my record, and told myself I had learned my lesson.

Years later—my last year and last semester of college to be exact—the devil tricked me again. I guess he thought since the last time he didn't ruin my life and my career, he was going to try one more time. And of course, I fell for his tricks again. If you think you have passed the test and learned your lesson, God will allow you to be tested just to make sure you will pass the test of time. Needless to say, I failed with flying colors. I had taken my younger brother to Orlando for spring break, and on our way back we stopped at the mall. He went to the men's department, and I went to the women's. I saw these expensive pants that I really wanted, but I didn't want to pay the money for them. So I thought that I would be able to get away with not paying for them since it was only one item, and I had just bought clothes for my brother. As soon as we got ready to leave the store, we were approached by store security. I felt so bad because my brother had no idea what was going on. We were taken into a room and questioned together, and that's when I realized that this is a serious problem. My actions could have ruined my brother's life. I told them he did not know what was going on and he was only 13 years old (even though he didn't look like it), so they let him go outside while they dealt with me. I really thought that I was going to go to jail because if you commit the same crime three times, it is considered a felony charge. As I set in the back of the police car, my brother sat outside the car looking at me, and all I could think was, "It's a wrap!" I thought that God had already given me two chances and that he was finished giving out chances. I didn't know how my brother was going to get home; I just knew I was going to have to tell my mom about this time and the other two, that I wasn't going to be able to graduate in two months, and even if I did graduate I definitely would not get a job in the business field with a felony. As I sat there, I started to pray, I asked God to please get me out of this one more time. I know that I had messed up but I really needed a miracle.

Even when it didn't look like He was going to come through, He did! I just so happened to get an inexperienced cop. He failed to see if I had any prior charges, but since he didn't look it up he released me and gave me a notice to appear in court. I couldn't believe it. I really thought I was going to have to sit in jail until my court date more than a month away. I learned that day, that Grace and Mercy is sho'nuff for real.

During that month, I researched attorneys because I knew I was going to need some representation to get me out of this. To get an attorney I needed some money, like thousands of dollars. I borrowed the money from a friend, but for some reason I was never released in my spirit to pay the attorney so he could start my case. One day I began to cry; I think I was crying out of fear and disappointment in myself. At the very moment my mom called me, asking me what was wrong because I fell on her spirit. I didn't want to tell her, but after hours of going back and forth I told her everything. She began to pray and tell me that everything was going to be fine. She said not to get the attorney and allow God to be my attorney.

When the time came, she went with me to court and told me to just watch and see that God had me. When my name was finally called, I went before the judge, and he asked me what was my plea. I pleaded no contest, and he gave me deferred prosecution— in other words another diversion program. I could not believe it! You are only supposed to get the diversion program one time in life. I was facing a felony charge where I could have been in jail for up to five years, and God gave me another chance. I am a true witness that He is a God of one, two and three chances. I completed the program; the charge was dismissed and removed from my record. I graduated with my Masters of Business Administration with honors and accepted a job with the State of Florida. Look at God!

Lessons Learned: So many valuable lessons were learned through that experience. My faith in the power of God increased tremendously. I realized the depth of a mother's love and the loyalty of a loving brother.

The devil thought he had me, but God had me covered. My origin, my family, and my history they all show that God's plan is tremendous. God has the power to make us live or die. Why aren't you in jail or dead yet? Because on God's agenda, your name is written down for something specific. The devil is not disturbed by whatever you have accomplished so far in your life; he is disturbed by your potential, the glimpse that God has given him of what you are going to do. The devil knows he cannot touch your future! When God sets you apart, there is always turbulence before calmness. When people stop talking about you, you are losing your edge.

The devil will use people who are close to you and know you. He knows that he cannot use a random stranger, somebody that is unfamiliar with you. The devil is smart enough to know that he has to use someone who has an opening in their lives for him. He will use your friends, family and spouse to try to destroy you. Tell the devil right now, "Devil, your plans have been interrupted. Plans cancelled!"

NOTES

_____

_____

_____

_____

_____

CHAPTER

LOVERS AND FRIENDS

When a situation seems too good
to be true, it usually is.

⊙his chapter of my life has evolved over 15 years. A long time ago, I made "the list" of everything I wanted in a man and my future husband. Of course, that list was edited and revised over time, however this boy, now man—or should I say grown boy—fit most of it (so I thought). I met "Matt" when I was ten years old, and he was thirteen, at an event of an organization that we were both apart of. He actually met my mom first and was trying to holla at her, lol, so she told him she had a daughter his age. She introduced us, and from there we became life-long friends and eventually lovers. He lived about an hour from me, so he would come to visit every weekend. He was there so much that he got a job at Subway in my hometown to validate him coming back and forth. We were truly best friends. When I was in the eighth grade, he invited me to his junior prom, and of course I went. My mom drove me and followed us around the whole night. We use to always joke about that night because the bold child that I was made him take my mom on a high-speed chase. Meanwhile, his girlfriend or ex-girlfriend (I don't really know what she was at the time), was in town and my mom ran into her at the gas station. So at one point, both my mom and this girl were trying to find us. Needless to say, I had a great time at the prom, riding around, and spending time together before I went back home.

Matt and I had so many great memories growing up. From prom to staying at my house (in another room of course, with my mom sleeping on the floor between the rooms, lol). Matt was always a part of my life through my first boyfriend, my first heartbreak, my dad, everything. We grew up together. When he graduated from high school, he moved to Tallahassee and attended FAMU. During that time I was in high school, in my first real relationship, rebelling against everything and everybody and totally all mixed up. We were not in touch that much and eventually he went into the Army.

When I graduated early and moved to Tallahassee to attend FAMU, we got back in touch with each other. He was stationed in Korea at the time, and I was a freshman living in the dorms, finally on my own. We began to communicate more often than before via phone cards, emails, and messenger webcam. He had a leave for the holidays, and as soon as he got home we were inseparable. I was no longer with my high school boyfriend but at a place where I was exploring the world and my options. He came home; we went back and forth between his hometown and Tally for me to go to class. I was really close with his mom and family. We spent a lot of time together and eventually had sex for the first time. Even though I had known him for so long, we never crossed the sexual line. He was the second person I had sex with. Now looking back, I don't know why I chose to do it at that time with him going back to Korea soon, but I did. So, of course I took it as we were together in an exclusive relationship since we had sex, right? Boy, was I wrong. Major red flags began to appear, but I was so young and naive that I failed to see them. Maybe because I did not even know what they were at the time or what they meant.

He left and returned to Korea. Of course, after having sexual intercourse with him I became even more attached. We would talk on the phone and email frequently. Eventually I noticed a change, as he became distant. We did not talk as much, and when we did talk conversations were short and irrelevant. One day I received an email from him telling me that he still had feelings for his ex and even though they are probably not getting back together he did not want to lead me on . . . yadda yadda yadda. The typical it's-not-you-it's-me speech. I was hurt, disappointed and did not know what to make of this email. I responded with my feelings, and things were never really the same after that.

We had plans to have a cookout when he returned home and of course the hopeful romantic that I am, I thought he would still invite me to come and hang out with the family. Boy, was I wrong again! I was informed by his cousin that he flew into his ex-girlfriend's city and rented a car, and the both of them drove to his hometown. The ex-now-current-girlfriend was in attendance at the cookout (that I planned!). This negro never even called to say he made it back in the States safely.

This was probably the beginning of the pain inflicted by him that had a negative effect on my life and heart. I locked myself in my first apartment (that I rushed to get so he would have somewhere instead of the dorms to stay when he returned) and cried until I could not cry anymore. I could not eat, sleep, nothing! His cousin was calling me telling me everything that was going on at the cookout, them going to the movies, etc. When I just could not take it anymore, I drove to his hometown an hour away and just drove by his house numerous times as I listened to Mariah Carey "We Belong Together." I can remember crying and singing. That was supposed to be me at that house with the family, why did he choose her? So many questions ran through my head, and I almost went and knocked on the door for answers, but I just could not do it. So I drove home with Mariah Carey's, "Shake it Off" on repeat.

After that heartbreak, I was not mature enough to learn whatever lesson I was supposed to learn and let go. Instead, I somehow found myself with another guy, who occupied my time in unhealthy ways. Looking back, I was numb to the pain and did not know or even care about what I was doing. He was a nice, older guy who persistently pursued me, and I was attracted to him, however, during that dark time in my life he was just that—"a nice, older guy who persistently pursued me" and who was in the right place at the right time. I really cannot recall how I made it through that heartbreak, but eventually it was over.

I did not talk to Matt for almost a year after that incident until I received a call from the infamous "bearer of bad news" cousin informing me that Matt was getting married to the girl that he ditched me for a year ago. I could not believe it. Yep, they were getting married that weekend. I feel back into deep depression, back to a place that I thought I was free from. God had already arranged for me to be out of town that weekend, just so I could not be that person that had something to say when the pastor asked if anyone objects to the union. Boarding that plane to Tennessee took every ounce of me, knowing that when I left I would have no way to just so happen end up at the wedding. God definitely knew what was best. When I returned home that following week, I received a phone call from Matt asking me "Did I call him?" I wanted to respond by saying "Hell no!" but instead I politely said, "No, I did not." There was a pause, so I proceeded to say congratulations. He said thank you, which confirmed it was really true, that I was not having a cruel nightmare. I had nothing else to say, and he seemed to have something to say but did not know how, so I said it for him. Goodbye.

MEN ARE GOLD DIGGERS, TOO

Men are always claiming that women are gold diggers and we are looking for a come up, on the prowl to find a man with a good job, owns a home, nice car, good credit, no children and no baby mama drama. That assumption is partially true. There are women who seek men with those prerequisites. However, there are also men who seek the same qualifications in women. Being a woman who lives a luxurious, comfortable lifestyle and not depending on a man to take care of me financially, there have been times where I have been pimped. Yes! You read right, pimped by a gold digging man.

Now, I am going to be nice enough to not put all the blame on the men. There is an epidemic with African American women who are gainfully employed, educated and financially secure. Oftentimes, us women are so focused on moving up the corporate ladder and securing a comfortable lifestyle for ourselves that we neglect to put forth the same energy in our personal lives. We have the big house, nice car and money in the bank with no one to share it with. The men that are of the same caliber are either married, intimidated by our success, and prefer a woman who has nothing, or are lifetime bachelors. So what do we do? Settle for the unemployed, broke, grown boy living at home with his momma that shows us a little attention and treats us nice with *our* money. One of my best friends has the "no good syndrome" and continues to date the same trifling guys over and over again. She is intelligent, successful career, makes a substantial amount of money and always seems to attract the guys who have multiple children, baby mama drama, and their momma's name tattooed on their neck lol (the tattoo may be an exaggeration, but everything else is pretty accurate). Each relationship, she finds herself taking care of these men and their children, dealing with unnecessary drama, and financing the relationship. I'm not dissing her because I have found myself in similar situations one time too many.

There was this one time with Matt. He was unemployed, had blown all of his inheritance, and broke. Of course, I felt bad for him and made the poor choice to take him in like an abandoned puppy. He came to stay with me while I was living in Cincinnati, and I was the sole provider. I gave him money, bought the food and cooked it, paid his cell phone bills, and even paid for him to get back in college. As I think back on this, all I can say is I was doing too much. In my defense, I did it because I know if I was in the same situation he would have done it for me, and there have been times when he bailed me out (literally). However, my issue was not me helping him, it was more so his motives and him being manipulative. Most men do not want to depend on a woman for anything, which I applaud. But with this particular situation, he was gold digging, and his intent was to use me for my money. In my besties situations, these dudes knew exactly what they were doing. Pimpin! Like I always say, men can only do what women allow them to do.

Lesson Learned: Do not allow men to use you! We have all put too much energy and resources into some relationships. However, relationships are a two-way street. Each person should give and receive. There has to be a balance. Marriage is an exception to the rule. When you're married, you're one. What's yours is mine. The only person that should have the benefit of receiving all of you is your spouse. If they have not said for richer or poorer, than you should not go broke taking care of them.

POTENTIAL

Why is it that women fall in love or stay in love with a man for their potential? Do we really believe enough in them to think that what is in front of us is going to change so drastically that we will have the perfect man? This is a problem I use to have and made excuses for myself saying that I am in the person's life to help them fulfill their potential and be the successful man they are supposed to be. Yeah, it all sounds good, but after a few lessons learned, I learned that when someone shows you who they really are, believe them. Don't sit there and continue kissing the frog thinking that he will become your prince. If he didn't transform after the first kiss, then you are simply just kissing a frog. And believe me, I have kissed too many frogs too many times thinking one of them would eventually change into my prince. You would think by now, I would be tired of kissing frogs, right? Nope. I've learned that there are many breeds of frogs out there; some of their warts were not as visible as others. For example, my first real boyfriend, I just knew that he had the potential to make it to the NBA and be the next LeBron James. Making me a true "Basketball Wife." He was talented and had the physical physique and strategic mind to be a great basketball player. However, he did not have the discipline, drive or determination to reach for his goals and change his lifestyle. Instead, he dropped out of community college, returned home to the streets, sold drugs, and eventually was murdered. This example may be a little extreme, but it's real. Regardless of how much I did to get him into college, do his work, and try to help him change, he had to want to change.

Another frog with potential, Matt was spoiled growing up, his mom gave him everything he wanted crippling him to never learn real responsibility. He grew up but did not mature into a man. Unfortunately, his mom passed away, leaving him a nice inheritance. I saw great potential in him to finish college, become a businessman, maintaining and investing the inheritance he was given. But instead, he blew it. In a matter of two years or less, everything was gone, no matter how hard I tried to help him realize the destructive mistakes he was making, all the while putting my heart on the line, too. He could not see it. Instead, he hurt me, hurt himself, and made poor decisions. When you are on the outside looking in, you can see much clearer. In his case, he was still trying to find his way, clean up the mess he has made, and get his life together. I loved him for the great potential he had, but you can't help someone who doesn't want to help themselves.

Joe had so much potential that I was willing to go through the ups and down to see it come to pass. I spoke into his life daily, prophesied all the things that I knew God had showed me for his life. Even in his present situation, he did not have a degree of higher education, worked deadbeat jobs, sold drugs, and rebelled against the call God had for his life. For some reason, I never really saw that person. The person I saw was a practical preacher/teacher using his life and testimony to reach the thugs on the streets, attracting women to God with his swag and personality, delivering a well-researched, biblically sound message in a different way. He loved to read the

Bible and pray, even when his lifestyle may not have resembled that of Christ. Deep down, I always saw the great potential he had and wanted to do anything I could to make it happen. I believed in him more than he believed in himself. I loved him beyond who he was, to who I knew he could be. He never thought he was good enough for me or that I could do better, and I tried to convince him otherwise. That's the problem with loving someone for their potential—if they don't make steps toward changing potential into reality, they will always be a frog. Potential must eventually lead to progress.

NOTES

_____

_____

_____

_____

_____

_____

CHAPTER

GOD KEPT ME

(Even when I didn't want to be kept)

Have you ever been in a place where you begin to blame God for your life being in shambles? Well, that is exactly where I found myself. I was so mad at God because I felt like it was His fault that all of my relationships had failed, that I had no money, that I did not have the career that I desired, that I was not driving the car that I wanted, and many, many other things. I just could not believe that out of all of my prayers, He chose to answer this one I made out of desperation "for the hidden things to be revealed and not my will but Your will be done." Ya'll better watch what you pray for, because God may just give you exactly that—good or bad.

I was so upset with God that I decided I wasn't going to pray anymore. I didn't want to hear anything else He had to say. In my opinion, He had said enough. I knew I was dead wrong, but I felt like God had done me wrong. God and I were not on good terms. I would talk to people and when they began to talk about God, the Bible or church I honestly did not want to hear it. I knew that was nothing but the devil, but I didn't care. Now I see how easy it is to fall into a reprobate mind and deny Christ. Most Christians would say they would never turn against God and deny Christ, but let me tell you, when you get into some rough situations and the more you pray and call to God for help, the worse those situations get. You begin to do a lot of things you said you would never do.

The more I tried to run away from God and just figure things out on my own, the more He ran after me. I felt like God was telling me "I am not going to let you go." The more He pulled, the more I bucked, kicked, screamed, ran, yelled and cried. I just did not want to give in; my flesh did not want to die. I didn't know it at the time, but there was a war going on between my spirit and my flesh. The struggle that I was going through prevented my spirit to rise above my flesh. My flesh was so accustomed to ruling that it did not want to go back under submission, and my spirit was saying that it had come too far to go back. My spirit had finally outgrown my flesh. The harder I fought, the harder the struggle became.

Even though I did not want to talk to God, He had me in a place to hear His Word one way or another. I began to listen to "my Bishop" as I affectionately call him on YouTube and God directed me to listen to messages that spoke to me right where I was. I began to study His Word and found myself gaining revelation and knowledge that only could have come from Him. He was showing me that I had to go through those things in order to gain a deeper understanding of who He is. God was trying to move me into a new season, but before He moved me, He had to purge me. I was led to read Revelation 3:8-10: *"I know all the things you do, and I have opened a door for you that no one can close. You have little strength, yet you obeyed my word and did not deny me. **9** Look, I will force those who belong to Satan's synagogue—those liars who say they are Jews but are not—to come and bow down at your feet. They will acknowledge that you are the ones I love. **10** Because you have obeyed my command to persevere, I will protect you from the great time of testing that will come upon the whole world to test those who belong to this world."*

What God was about to do in my life was not because of my qualifications or me. I was nowhere near qualified (Ya'll read the chapter "Who Would Have Thought."). I had to realize that I am not qualified, but I am chosen. So stop tripping about all the stuff you have done and what didn't go right in your life. Just know that when God chooses you, nothing else matters. God says to give Him the opportunity to show you what you have never seen before. He has set before you an open door that no one can shut. It no longer matters who likes you or not because guess what? They cannot shut the door! Your greatest enemy cannot shut it. Who cares? It's too late for all of that. Like I always say, "The devil should have killed me when he had me, but he messed up when he let me go." I refuse to lose sleep or stress out because God has chosen me and opened a door before me that no man can shut. If God has allowed for me to still be breathing after all of the many things I have gone through, then I know that I know that I know that He has to have a plan and purpose for my life. Whatever He has planned must be big because the devil has been fighting me hard since birth. He must know something I don't know, but what I do know is that I'm ready to walk through the open door!

Lessons Learned: Even through the storm, my life took on a new focus. My faith increased, my love for God became deeper, and I realized the importance of following the plan of God. Don't buck, don't fight, just adjust yourself and allow God to reposition your life. You have to know what to ignore. Don't get mad at God. Get mad at the devil. Learn to make your obstacles work for you. Get ready to walk through the doors that God has opened for you.

NOTES

_____

_____

CHAPTER

THE RELATIONSHIP FROM HELL . . . LITERALLY

"For I know the plans I have for you,' says the Lord.
'They are plans for good and not for disaster, to give
you a future and a hope. [12] *In those days when you pray,*
I will listen. [13] *If you look for me wholeheartedly, you*
will find me. [14] *I will be found by you,' says the Lord. 'I*
will end your captivity and restore your fortunes. I will
gather you out of the nations where I sent you and will
bring you home again to your own land."

Jeremiah 29:11

People say that the devil comes in sheep's clothing. Well not this devil. He came to me looking just like the ol' ugly wolf he was. And for some crazy reason I chose to accept this ol' wolf thinking I could upgrade him (lol). So it all started during my college graduation weekend. I went to a nightclub to celebrate. As I am having a good time with friends and fellow graduates, I am pulled to the side by this guy (Let's just call him "Joe"). He says, "What's up Raevyn?" His face looks familiar, but I didn't really know who he was. He said I'm "Joe," I vaguely remembered who he was, we talked, exchanged numbers, and continued on with our night. After the club closed, I received a text message from Joe saying it was nice seeing me and he was having a cookout the next day, and I should stop by. I said I would think about it and said good night.

 To make an entirely too long of a story short, we went to lunch on the day of my graduation. He came to my graduation, and we were inseparable from then. Some background on Joe: I knew him when I was younger, our churches use to affiliate with each other, and his parents were pastors. As we begin to spend time together, the friendship seemed so comfortable and right. We didn't have to force anything, we liked some of the same things, we were both brought up in the church, parents are in the ministry, etc. On the flip side, he wasn't my physical type at all, his financial and educational status weren't up to par, and his style of dress just was not what I was used to.

 RED FLAG: When you are in the beginning stages of getting to know someone as a potential mate and you observe a number of things that do not meet your criteria, RUN! RUN FAST and FAR!

Do not stay and take them on as a project, thinking you can change them or upgrade them; it's probably not going to happen. And definitely do not stay and change your criteria instead. Because when you do, you change your standards, and when you change your standards you are allowing that other person to dictate what you want. "If you don't stand for something, you will fall for anything," which means you will just settle for any ol' thang. You are worth more than any ol' thang.

Ok, back to "Joe." So we met in May, and by June we were practically living together. The crazy thing is ever since my freshman year in college, I was determined to move to Atlanta when I graduated. When I graduated, I was packed and ready to move, and then all hell broke loose (literally). The job I had in Atlanta pushed back my start date, I didn't have any money, and I was about to be evicted from my apartment ("Who Would Have Thought?" That's another chapter). So I moved my stuff to Joe's place until I figured out what in the world I was going to do. I was living with this guy I just started talking to, no job, no money and lost. One morning I got up went outside and opened the Bible. I opened it to Jeremiah 29:11, which reads *"For I know the plans I have for you,' says the Lord. 'They are plans for good and not for disaster, to give you a future and a hope. [12] In those days when you pray, I will listen. [13] If you look for me wholeheartedly, you will find me. [14] I will be found by you,' says the Lord. 'I will end your captivity and restore your fortunes. I will gather you out of the nations where I sent you and will bring you home again to your own land."*

When I read the scripture, I broke into tears. God was telling me that He knows the plans He had for me, I just needed to look for him wholeheartedly, and that's what I did. I prayed and asked for His guidance. I didn't know what to do; all I knew is that me shacking up, being broke, and doing nothing with my life wasn't it. I prayed and was led to call my mom. I told her about the scripture and how I was feeling. Before I knew it, I was telling her that I was coming home. I didn't know where that was coming from because I knew it wasn't Raevyn at all. Everybody that knows me knows that I do not like Apalachicola and stay as far from there as possible. So I knew God was sending me home for a reason. What that reason was, I had no clue, I just knew I needed to go. I packed my stuff that day and told Joe I was going home.

I went to Apalach and God had a job waiting on me with a summer program. Another "Who Would Have Thought" moment—me back in Apalach with my Masters of Business Administration degree working with kids at a summer program. I felt like I was going through hell on earth! I would wake up, go to work, go home and sleep until time for me to go to work the next day. I was miserable to say the least. The only thing I had to look forward to was getting off work on Thursday and driving to Tallahassee to spend the weekend with Joe. Our summer weekends were great! We spent quality time together, went out with friends, hosted get-togethers at his house, took dance classes, cooking classes and anything else there was to do in Tallahassee. In my mind's fairy tale, I thought my relationship was the only thing that was good in my life at the time.

One night at church I received a prophecy from an out of town prophet telling me she saw me trying to make a decision between two guys and she wanted me to know that God said neither one of them was "the one." I could have fallen out right then and there.

I just knew for sure that Joe was the one. He was a Christian, brought up in the church, and truly loved God. I dismissed her word and said she was a false prophet because I just knew this was my husband. I tell ya, how foolish we are when we don't know the whole plan God had for us. I continued the relationship with Joe; we talked about marriage and wedding plans. The summer program ended, and I decided to fast and pray for two days to hear from God for my next move. I really wanted to go to Atlanta, but I didn't have a job there. I fasted and prayed and thought that God told me to go to Atlanta on faith and trust, that He will work everything out when I got there. I just had to go. I packed all of my things in my car and was on my way. I made a pit stop in Tallahassee to see Joe and tell him my plans. He didn't want me to go, but he didn't want to hold me back either. What was supposed to be a couple days spending time with the boo turned into me not moving to Atlanta. I still don't know why I never left, all I know is that I was living in Tallahassee with my boyfriend.

I began to look for jobs in Tallahassee, and after a few weeks of looking I got a job with the State of Florida Unemployment Office (go figure). After about a month, I was promoted. I began to think that promotion was a sign that I was where I was supposed to be. So wrong! I became content in my situation, environment and relationship. However, my picture-perfect relationship began to change. Joe and I didn't really talk to each other anymore; we would just walk around the house and not speak. I just began to sleep (which is my way of escape). It seemed like the honeymoon phase was over before it had even *legally* started. As I look back, I don't know where it all began to go wrong; actually I do know—at the beginning. It was never meant to be in the first place. I know that love is blind, but the devil had me both blind and death. I had eligible and not-so-eligible guys trying to holla at me, and I was so stuck on stupid. I thought the more I did for him, would keep him. Lord, was I wrong. I actually think it pushed him farther away. We went from planning the wedding to let's give it a little more time.

Joe decided to take a weekend getaway to Atlanta. I didn't think it was a good time with the state of our relationship. He chose to go, and I chose to break up with him (immature, I know). When he got back, he brought back the "old Joe." The old Joe is the playa, secretive, liar, unfaithful, not the boyfriend-type Joe. The representative was now gone, and the true person was now present. Another prophet spoke into my life and said to pray that all hidden things regarding my relationship would be revealed. I prayed that prayer and within a week too much was revealed, and I could not handle it. That wolf in sheep clothing came out in full force! I tell ya, be careful what you pray for because God may just answer your prayers. The first thing God revealed was not clear enough for me. I was out of town and had a woman's intuition. I just had that feeling that this negro was about to try me, and sho'nuff he did. He had an unknown visitor at his house and for some strange reason chose not to answer the phone or reply to text messages. Side note: Fellas, if you are cheating or doing something you have no business doing, let me help you out: Don't break routine! And by that I mean, females observe and learn your routine and habits. When you begin to break or change them, your actions are obvious that something is not right. From my experience, a woman's intuition is usually 99.9% correct (I'm just saying).

Ok back to the revealing. When I could not get in touch with Joe I sent a friend to his house. Joe chose not to come to the door.

After hours had passed, I finally received a phone call from him. When I answered the phone, he immediately asked me if I had ever had an abortion. What?! The old diversion tactic. My dumb butt actually fell for it. I asked him what was he talking about and was this really relevant right now? Bargaining to address the more important matter at hand, which was who the hell (excuse my language, I was saved but not delivered) was at his house and why was he ignoring my calls and texts. He proceeded to lie— poorly if I say so myself—saying that he wasn't home, and he let a "friend" use his house. Really? Did he really think I was going to believe that ish? I asked him who and he says someone from out of town. Ok. I guess he thought I was boo boo the fool. Whatever! Then he asked me again about the abortion. I could have continued to follow the current trend and lie, but for what? At this point, I felt like I was literally about to lose my mind. So I told the truth and said yes. Now, this cheating, lying negro has the nerve to question me. When? Only one? What happened? Oh, so now you want to talk, but for the past three hours you didn't want to answer your phone? Still, I told him about the abortions, having his full attention.

The truth was I found myself in high school, in love and pregnant from Ray (my first). I knew that we were not ready to parent a child. After much prayer and thought, I made one of the hardest decisions of my life: to terminate the pregnancy. My only slight comfort was a scripture in Ecclesiastes 3:3 that said there is a time to kill and a time to heal. Not sure if I was taking this scripture out of context, but I repented and prayed for God's forgiveness. A year or so later, I became pregnant again. I thought I had learned my lesson the first time, but it obviously takes me a time or two to learn lessons the hard way. I was in college, and Ray was still on the streets. Not much had changed since the last time. I made another difficult decision to terminate the pregnancy and to permanently terminate our relationship. Ray was my first love, my first sexual partner, and my best friend. The soul tie needed to be broken indefinitely. Once we decided not to get married, it was best we moved on with our lives.

Lesson Learned: During this time in my life, God showed me His unconditional love and forgiveness. I had made some very bad choices in life at an early age, but God was still there to comfort me. I always thought I would allow the abortions to be skeletons in my closet never to come out. But the devil is liar! He will NOT keep me in bondage! Skeletons represent something dead. Those skeletons are dead and will no longer hold me hostage to my past. I didn't know it then, but God was calling me to a ministry of true repentance, redemption and restoration.

Back to the story. Once I told Joe everything he responded by telling me that he didn't know if we were going to be able to move forward with our relationship and if he would ever be able to trust me again. You trust me?! Chile please. I never lied to him, just finished telling him the truth about something that no one knew about me not even my best friend and he felt betrayed? Pause. Isn't he the same person that just lied to me and still hasn't told me where he was, who was at his house and why he didn't answer my call? Exactly. Anywho, the conversation ended, even though it wasn't over.

The nightmare was only beginning . . . The next morning I flew back to Tally, ending my trip early without him knowing, and had my bff pick me up at the airport and drive directly to his house. When we pulled up, he was not home. I walked in the house, and it seemed as if he hasn't been there, and from the looks of things didn't stay there the night before. I literally go on a witch hunt to find him. I drove to his parents' house and find his car and the unknown vehicle parked in the driveway. Everything in me wanted to knock on the door, but I couldn't. I sat outside, lights off, and just wondered, "Who does this car belong to and what are they doing in the house?" I called a police officer friend of mine and had him run the tag of the car. He provided me with the owner's name, and of course my speculation was correct. It was a female. Not some homeboy's friend from out of town but his side boo that lived locally. I tried to plan my next move, and all I could do was gather enough strength to put my car in drive and drive home. I cried myself to sleep.

The next day, I decided to confront him and ask who the girl was. I gave him one last chance to be honest and hopefully help me to let go. He said that she was an old friend. That was partially true, but who is this girl to you? He wouldn't answer any other questions. As the next few days went by, I was basically a stalker, lol. I would drive by his house multiple times a day and this trick—I mean girl's—car would be there. Each time I would see her car, a small part of me would die. I was hurt, angry and eventually became a woman scorned. When I allowed myself to become a mad black woman is when I snapped. I've watched movies when the woman has snapped on her husband or boyfriend and cheered her through the screen. This time it wasn't a movie. It was my reality; I had my first Angela Basset from "Waiting to Exhale" moment. I didn't burn up all of his belongings and car.

However, I did mess up a few things and inconvenienced his life a little. My mom once told me that hurt people want to hurt people. And that's just what I did, shared the pain I feeling emotionally with him materially.

My breaking point was one morning I went to his house before I went to work to take him breakfast. We had talked the night before, worked things out and all was better. So I thought. When I arrived at his house, the girl's car was there. I checked the car and it seemed as if the car had been there overnight. I politely knocked on the door, and no one answered. I called his phone, and he did not answer. I went to his bedroom window and knocked (more like banged) and still no response. So I sat in my car in the driveway and was determined that I was not going to leave or move my car, which was blocking them both in, until someone came out of this house. All kinds of thoughts ran through my mind. I knew that this could become my first snapped episode. I believed that my love was too passionately fatal to be thrown back in my face. Eventually the door opened and this mystery girl exits the house, as Joe escorts her to her car. I pulled my car over to the side and walked into the house. We had a heated argument about why is she staying the night at his house if she was just a "friend" and he continued to spew lie after life. It took that incident for me to realize my worth. I looked like a pure fool fighting for a relationship and man that didn't love me. It was obvious Joe did not love me. His actions showed that he was not the one for me. After all of that I finally got it. Closure did not come instantly. The wounds were left open, yet the relationship had ended. I guess that's the real meaning of open-ended.

Lesson Learned:

Don't settle for something just because you think it's the best you can get or something that may be the best for someone else. Always remember that God knows the plans He has for you; they are plans for good and not for disaster, to give you a future and a hope. Don't you know that God will not have a plan for you that is lame? His plan will be the bomb, the best! Take heed to warnings! Warnings come before destruction. When God is trying to get a point across He will, one way or another. Take it from me, God's way is far better than your own. Always trust your gut feelings. When you feel like something is wrong, do a little research before assuming or jumping to conclusion. I want to warn you first, don't go looking for something that you are not ready to find! If you do happen to find something be prepared to handle the situation in a manner where you will not have any regrets. "Don't regret what you do, regret what you don't do."

BREAKING POINT

Keri Hilson has a song, "Breaking Point," in which she sings, "Every woman has a breaking point ya'll . . . some woman can be lied to, cheated on and beated on." What is your breaking point? You know, that one thing that when it is done to you, regardless how much you love that person you are done? Men and women are often different in this area. A woman can be cheated on time and time again and she still takes the man back because she loooooves him. Now let a chick cheat on a dude. It's a wrap! There is not a conversation, apology, let's work on it. He is done! And if he stays in the relationship, believe me, he has tapped out emotionally. I've had this discussion with different men and women about why this is true. One dude said that it takes men longer to fall for a girl and completely let her in. So when he finally does, and she betrays him, it is too hard for him to get over it. Ok. I understand his perspective, and yes some women do fall faster than guys. However, the real question is "Why do women give guys another chance?" Once a cheater, always a cheater, right? Why do we set ourselves up to be hurt again? A girlfriend of mine answered the question by saying that women love harder than men, and we just don't want to let go so easily. Now I beg to differ with that statement. I do believe that women may fall in love faster, but harder? No. Yes, we do love hard, but I have learned from experience that when men finally fall in love, they love hard.

So, what do you do when every last one of your trigger points have been pushed and you are at your breaking point, but can't break?

This reminds me of when I was on the last stretch of my relationship with Joe. He had lied to me, cheated on me and took every ounce of pride and self-worth I had left in me. I once heard a quote, "If you can't save the relationship, save your pride." Well, my pride was gone out the window. For the first time, I was at my breaking point but didn't know how to let go. I had given my all and was facing the inevitable part of the movie that I dreaded and that was the end. Sometimes in life, you come to the point where you reach your breaking point, your *aha!* light bulb moment, and you walk away. Other times it only takes one small incident that reassures you it's time to move on. It could be a huge caught in the act moment or just one simple text message that gives you the push you need to let the credits roll and begin the next sequel.

CHEATING

Like probably every other woman in the world, I've been cheated on and have "technically" cheated on someone. My definition of cheating may be different than the next person's, though. I believe cheating is everything you wouldn't do in front of your significant other, such as inappropriate conversations, promiscuous texting, flirting, physical interactions and transactions, sex, etc. If my man wouldn't want me seeing a text message or overhearing his conversation with someone of the opposite sex, then I see that as cheating. The same goes for me. There have been times when I have been in a relationship and caught myself having inappropriate conversations with an old male friend and had to quickly nip things in the bud. Men are territorial and do not like for any man to try to holla at their woman. Why is it that men cheat and expect the chick to forgive them and take them back, but let a chick cheat? Oh it's a wrap! Men are gone and will not look back. This is such a double standard. Women need to flip the script and have the same tenacity and strength to move on when her man cheats. Some actions should not be excusable. What your man does not appreciate, believe me, another man will.

LIFE DOES NOT MAKE SENSE

The secret things belong unto the LORD our God: but those things which are revealed belong unto us and to our children forever, that we may do all the words of this law Deut. 29:29. My interpretation of this scripture is God simply telling us that sometimes life is not going to make sense. In most cases, it was not even designed to. God reveals things in His timing. If He was to show us our entire lives, we would freak out! I know I would. There have been times when I asked for God to reveal things to me, and when He did I could not handle it. I told you guys about the prayer that prophetess had me pray—"for all secret things to be revealed." Lord have mercy, some things are best left unrevealed, lol. Who said that we were supposed to know everything and that life is supposed to be this exact science? Some fool who doesn't trust in the all-knowing, ever present Creator, that's who. All we can do is let go, let God, and keep it moving.

The night that I was moving my things out of Joe's house, I felt as if I was going through a nasty divorce and had no clue where I was going to go or what I was going to do. I had my best friend, her brother, his wife and kids helping me move all of my furniture. Every piece of furniture that left that house felt like a piece of my heart leaving and being placed in a truck. Once the truck was all loaded up, everything inside of me wanted to set that house on fire. Like Angela Bassett in "Waiting to Exhale" and Lisa Left-Eye Lopez, I just wanted to see all his ish go up in flames. When the last item was loaded and I did my final walk through of the house, my mind was ticking like a bomb about to explode trying to think of a way to get back at Joe, to make him feel the pain that I felt at that very moment. My bestie was following me around the house because she knew that I was up to something. I told everyone they could go on over to the storage unit. They begin to leave the house, and my bestie decided that she would wait and ride with me. Since she decided to stay, I decided I wouldn't do anything right then, but he was not going to be let off that easy, he was going to feel my wrath.

My mom was on her way to Tally to make sure I was okay. She called me and asked where I was. I tried to sound sane, but she could read right through me. I was on the verge of a mental, physical and spiritual breakdown and needed to do something to release my pain. We met up in a parking lot when she saw me and said, "Rae, let it go, you are not yourself. I know you are hurting right now, but it is for the best." I continue to act a fool saying what I am going to do and he deserves to be hurt, too. She says four words to me that makes me shut up and listen, "hurt wants to hurt." When she said those words, I begin to breakdown and cry. He had hurt me so badly that all I wanted to do was to make him feel the hurt he had caused me. I didn't burn his house down, but after a few days had passed, let's just say I got him back and felt much better. Can't tell everything . . . something's have to go to the grave. Gotta protect the guilty in this case, even if it is me.

NEW YEAR'S EVE

A few months had passed, and I decided to travel to beautiful Miami for New Year's Eve. For some odd reason, I still could not get Joe off of my mind. I kept wondering why did the relationship end the way it did and if there was any way to fix it. I was up all night wishing we could work things out even though I knew we were not supposed to be together. You really can't help who you love.

I woke up one morning with him on my mind. I had done well the past month but I guess with my cycle about to start I was more emotional than usual. As I was driving, our song "The Best I Ever Had" came on the radio. Crazy! I'm like, "God, for real? You already know I cannot handle this right now. He wasn't the best I ever had or will have, but I do miss him." While I'm listening to the song, I receive an email from him. Wow! The email almost made me give in. The email read:

Before the New Year I just wanted to wish u a happy n blessed 2010. I know that u r focused and being productive. It is obvious that u want nothing to do or say to me n that I understand n respect. I would just like to thank you for your encouragement, motivation and all the change you brought into my life in 09. I really do appreciate what u meant to my life. Ppl say the greatest gift u can give some is to utilize the wisdom u learned from them, with that being the case I will continually utilize the things learned from u and try to be a better person. I apologize sincerely with no excuse of why things happen the way they did. I wish you the best in life and know that, "whatsoever u do shall prosper!" I will always love you and your family and will continue to pray for you and them. Have a great year and a great life.

P.S You are and will always be "The Best I Ever Had!"

Love,
Joe

With me already pre-pmsing and emotional, I could not handle it. I broke down! I don't know if this was God or the devil, but all I do know is that this is definitely not how I saw my life being. This was the holiday season from hell. I just prayed that 2010 would be far better than 2009.

In my distress, I talked to my godmother and asked for her advice. She asked if I thought that he was the best I could have. My answer was no. She said, "Well, if he's not then just let it go." She said I would be stupid to go back, that the only reason I would go back is because the one time I lowered my standards he didn't take the opportunity to have a good thing. He chose to be dumb and mess up the best he ever had. With that being the case, he did not deserve a second chance. If I went back, he probably would think he could do the same thing all over again. Her husband also spoke some powerful words. He said that God has given me the opportunity to graduate with my MBA, move to a wonderful city, and to work for one of the top three most prestigious accounting firms in the world. God gave me those opportunities, and if I went back then I was throwing those opportunities back in God's face. He said that I needed to control my emotions for a short period of time and then opportunities would open up. That stuck with me. If I can just control my emotions for a little while, then doors will open and more opportunities will come. He said that I deserved better, and that my ex was nothing but baggage—baggage that I didn't need and that can cause nothing but damage. Everything he said was a confirmation of what many family members, prophets and God has told me. All I needed was a reality check. Now I'm good and back to being strong!

Lesson Learned: Surround yourself with Godly people who love you enough to tell you what is best for you regardless of what excuses you are trying to make. If somebody loves you, make them work hard to get you back. Don't allow an email, text message or gift to draw you back in; he gotta come better than that. If you go back to someone that disrespected you, he will never respect you. If you leave and don't look back, they will always regret and realize what they lost. If a man is stupid enough to leave a Bentley or Rolls Royce for a 1962, rusted Volkswagen Beatle, then he does not deserve you. If he is dumb enough to not recognize or respect the treasure he has, then he does not deserve you. Either way he is stupid and not worthy of you. Going back to someone that means you no good and is nothing but extra baggage adds nothing to your self-worth. If anything, he is devaluing who you are. Know your worth!

HOMECOMING—HOME GOING

As I approached Tallahassee city limits my excitement turned into depression. Feelings of hurt, pain, confusion, hatred and anger all flood my mind as I drove into the city that once was my home, but now I referred to it as hell or at least the suburbs of hell. I returned to the "burbs" for what was supposed to be a joyous occasion . . . FAMU Homecoming! It's a time where are the current students and alums come together to catch up with old friends, classmates, sorors and ex's, a time to find out what everyone is doing with their lives and how successful they have become. I have been attending homecoming since I can remember, from being carried in my mom's stomach and arms, to being chaperoned as I tried to be grown, to being a true Rattler that bleeds orange and green and now as an alumnus of the illustrious Florida Agriculture and Mechanical University. The only good memory I have of Tallahassee is the five years I spent there in college. College was definitely a great time in my life. A time that I will always remember and frequently refer back to. The people I met, some who became lifelong friends and others who will just be a place to stay all over the world. The experiences, the memories and the life-long lessons always will be cherished.

That weekend, I subconsciously hoped not to run into Matt or Joe. I felt like I wasn't emotionally ready to face either of them. It had been almost five months since I had seen Joe and two months since I had seen Matt. Given the way things ended with both of them, I just thought it would be best not to reignite any feelings or emotions, negative or positive. I had my bestie with me, and I really just wanted to have a good time, however the more I tried, the more everything reminded me of one of the guys. As the weekend commenced, I ran into old flames, the welcoming was warm, and it was genuinely good to see everyone. I just wished that I could feel the same way about Matt and Joe as I did these other men that were once a part of my life. Throughout the entire weekend, I just really couldn't enjoy myself like I usually did.

I went into the weekend with as much optimism that I could possibly muster in my emotional state. Friday was cool; I ran into a lot of old friends, old lovers and old crushes. On Saturday, my mom brought my brother and some of his friends up for the game. My mom asked me had I seen anybody on "my list." I said, "No and I probably won't." She said the weekend is not over yet so don't get too happy. She also said that she really believed that with as many people there are in Tallahassee and at homecoming that if I happened to be in the same place as somebody it would not be a coincidence. She began to explain that it's not a coincidence to be in the same place at the same time and with all the hundreds of people in that same place to manage to see that person. She told me if that did happen, that obviously God orchestrated for it to be that way. How I reacted to that orchestration was up to me.

So, Saturday night I met up with my girls and went to a party that was the typical FAMU Alum crowd. It was not a local club where just anybody would be. I was strategically trying to minimize my chances of running into any "locals." The night started off good; I was beginning to enjoy myself and not worry about what was going on inside. Little did I know that night was the grand finale that forced me in to dealing with all the feelings I had consciously and unconsciously suppressed for almost a year.

As I danced and began to have a good time one of my friends came up to me and said she just ran into Joe. In that moment, my heart started to beat harder and harder. I asked where, and she led me to the vicinity of where she saw him. We walked by as if we didn't see him, and yep in the flesh there was Joe. For some strange reason, I could not bring myself to speak to him. Why you might ask? Probably because I was obviously not over him. Let's keep it real; if I was over him I would have been able to walk up to him say hello maybe even give him a hug and go on about my night with no second thoughts. Sounds easy enough. However, in this situation, I was not capable of doing any of the above. I attempted to carry on with my night, but continued to coincidentally cross paths with him multiple times. Each time, I thought I had psyched myself out enough to be the "bigger person" by casually speaking and keep it moving. Unfortunately, each time I would play the game and act as if I did not see him. When the night finally came to an end, I felt defeated and confused. I thought I had found closure with him, but it was apparent there were unaddressed feelings still lingering. Seeing Joe was like hearing an old song on the radio, taking you right back to where you were when you first heard it and all the memories that were made from it, a tune and lyrics that you cannot drown out.

A month after homecoming, I still hadn't got back right, either mentally or emotionally. I tell ya, my emotions were having the highest highs and lowest lows. I was at the point where I didn't know if I was coming or going. I was focused and driven in my career, more than ever. However, it seemed like I couldn't convince myself that I was truly internally happy and fulfilled. Don't get it twisted, I am not saying that I needed a man to be happy and fulfilled, that's definitely NOT the case. I was just in the process of learning to accept the season that God had me in and make the best out of it.

I noticed myself subconsciously embracing the new life and mindset I had, however I felt like I suppressed a part of my life that I had not yet totally dealt with and healed from. I consider myself a strong individual who can take a lickin and keep on tickin; unfortunately my way in going about keeping it moving is all wrong and definitely not healthy. I either hold it all in, replace it with something or someone else, suppress it, conscious denial and experimenting with things completely out of my character. The harder I tried to grow spiritually, the weaker I became to things that usually did not attract me. For example, one day I found myself smoking weed for the second time (The first time was with Joe when my dog Diva was killed by a car, then my car was stolen and wrecked.), I was high as a kite and got drunk on top of that . . . . in the middle of the week! I thought, *What in the world am I going through?!? Is this a quarter life crisis?* Then one time I went to the casino alone and gambled, losing $200 of money that I couldn't afford to lose. I used that lost as a reason to get drunk again and I was totally wasted and to continue the downward spiral I went out to a club, was totally loose, off the chain, all the way live and any other wild phrase you can think of to explain my demeanor. I ended up leaving the club with a guy I was talking to when I first moved to Tampa, needless to say a nightcap ensued thereafter (wasn't the first time), breaking my three months of celibacy. And to tell you the truth, it wasn't even good. Sin is never good and definitely not good for you. I was really too drunk and sleepy to even know what was going on. Not an excuse, just the humiliating truth. I woke up the next day nauseous, vomiting, head aching, and sick of myself. I was sick and tired of making poor decisions and having to go to God for forgiveness for the same things over and over. So I didn't. I was too embarrassed and ashamed to even go to God and say sorry. I was so disappointed in myself; how was I back in this place? Why couldn't I pass the test? When would I ever learn?

As I write this now, God is answering those questions. He is telling me we all fall short of the glory of God. You were born into sin, and sometimes things happen to show us that we are nothing without God. A just man falls seven times, get up! Repent and turn from your wicked ways. You can't just sit there and dwell in your shortcomings; you have to GET UP, dust yourself off, and continue the work God has for you.

Lesson Learned: Everyone makes mistakes, and just when you think you are over something, God will allow for it to come back just to show you that we are all a work in progress. We will be tested daily; for the ones we fail, go back get the answer key and be ready for the next test. It may not come as a multiple choice like the first one, but you can use the same information on an essay test.

NOTES

CHAPTER

FIGHTING A WAR IN STILETTOS

And so, after he had patiently endured, he obtained the
promise. For men verily swear by the greater: and an
oath for confirmation is to them an end of all strife.
Hebrews 6:15-16

When I finally realized that I was in the fight of my life, I had to prepare to win. I was tired of getting beat. I was fighting the enemy under my own, wrong power. Let me tell you, it is difficult to fight the enemy when you just finished sleeping with him. I found myself hanging out with the enemy one day and then trying to rebuke him the next day. It just doesn't work. That's why I was getting my butt beat. The enemy knows all of your weak points, where you are vulnerable and exactly what to offer you. He knew my weaknesses were men, relationships, companionship and love. He also knew exactly what my type was, the type of guy that would have me sprung in no time. Like my mommy always say, "Death by temptation." It is hard to fight someone you have been hugging, kissing and being intimate with. I'm not saying that you are physically fighting that person in the flesh (even though you probably want to); instead, you are fighting the spirit that is within that person.

The Bible says we wrestle not against flesh and blood but against principalities . . . That is why the enemy has to use all of his best tactics against us to try to win the fight because he knows that we are on the winning side. The enemy knows where to hit you. He will not offer you something you do not want. You have to ask God, how can I win? It's hard to win when you feel like every time you trust someone they leave or when you think you have found the right person they betray you. I heard someone say that if you want to know how to win every time, don't get in the ring because if you get in the ring with the devil he will knock you out. Instead, throw some scriptures into the ring and tell the devil that the battle is not mine it is the Lord's. I can do all things through Christ that strengthens me, greater is He that is within me than he that is within the world, God shall supply all my needs according to His riches and glory, Satan the blood of Jesus is against you. Rather than you fight the devil with will power, meditation, yoga and new age thinking, simply tell Satan, "The Lord rebuke thee!" Let him know that God is going to bring you out of this. Sometimes there is a feeling of being vulnerable or insecure when you are fighting someone that knows all of your weaknesses. This is the time you step aside and allow God to fight your battle. You are not ready for the level of warfare the devil is going to bring. He is going to attack your finances, relationships, your mind and body. When he pulls out all of his good tricks and machinery, he thinks he has you surrounded and goes in for the kill, but greater is He that is in you than he that is in the world!

Lessons Learned: Sometimes you have to get outright righteously indignant with the devil. Tell him he may have thought he won, but it is not over! You have more fight in you. The devil has stolen some things from you and he owes you your stuff! He hit you hard, but you want revenge! If he only knew what you were going to be, he would not have bothered you, because now you are stronger and wiser, you have more power, strength, anointing and favor. Tell the devil you want all of your stuff back—your family, your self-esteem, your joy, your peace, your destiny, everything! Take it back!

NEW BREED

Our generation is the new breed. We are bold enough to march toward the gates of the enemy. When we get to the gates, we have to be militant and take back everything the devil stole from us! We are a chosen generation, a royal priesthood, and we are armed and dangerous! The time has come for us to stand up, be strong and ready to fight the enemy. When we all come together and realize that it is not a black thing, white thing, rich thing or poor thing, but that it is a kingdom thing, we will be a force to be reckoned with.

THE DEVIL IS A LIAR!

I encourage you to look at your situation, whatever it may be—if you are about to be evicted from your apartment, your car repossessed, you are pregnant out of wedlock, you have had an abortion, you can't get over a failed relationship, you're a high school dropout or you just lost your job. Whatever your situation is I want you to look at it in its face and say THE DEVIL IS A LIAR! I don't care how bad it looks or how much you want to just give up. I was sent to tell you that the devil is a liar and he will not win! You have to get outright indignant with the devil, the same way you would if your boyfriend or girlfriend tried you. Let the devil know that you mean business. I'm good for telling the devil that he messed with the wrong one. I am crazy, and I will shoot a demon!

When the devil starts tripping and trying your life, that is when you know that God is about to open doors that have been restricted. Some people have denied you access just because of who you are. The enemy is not stupid; he knows that God cannot fail. He will perform and will always do what He says. As a child of God, you have been fighting some things that do not make sense. Just know that the enemy is not fighting you where you are, he's fighting where you are going. That's why the battle is so intense! Where you are going is off the chain! Hebrews 6:15-16 states, *And so, after he had patiently endured, he obtained the promise. For men verily swear by the greater: and an oath for confirmation is to them an end of all strife.* Stick it out! God is going to give you everything He promised. When God says it's your time, it is simply your time. You have to build your life on your prophetic future. When things are looking really bad in my life, I refer back to my prophecies. I read them, listen to them and declare that I will get everything that God promised me. I begin to prophecy to myself. The answer to your problem is to prophecy what God is saying. The devil only attacks something he is threatened by. Obviously he just does not like you and is trying his best to kill you. That's when you have to let him know that he should have kept you sorry and pitiful because now he slipped up and let you get enough sense and strength to snap out of your depression and realize that he is a liar! If you are going through a battle, that's a good thing, because you always face the biggest battle before your biggest breakthrough! So man up, fight, and BREAK THROUGH!

Lessons Learned: You are fighting unseen enemies like never before. Ask the Lord to anoint your head and feet and to send His angels to cover you while you are on the battleground. Once you really become tired of principalities attacking you and the devil stealing from you is when you become militant. Tell the devil that he will not take one more thing from you! Then take it back! Get ready for the battle! Get ready to win! You will not be defeated. The enemy will flee. Wage war against the enemy. Take back your territory! It's time. The devil cannot win, unless you let him. He cannot do anything to you without your permission.

"FOR RAEVYN"

One relaxing Saturday afternoon, I was in my most favorite place in the world, my comfy couch, watching "For Colored Girls who considered suicide when the rainbow is enough" by Tyler Perry. Now that title says a lot in itself. Almost sounds like the movie of my life, "For Raevyn, who considered suicide when the rainbow aka the promise wasn't enough." As black women, we have considered a lot of things when that man, job, child and anything else we have put our heart into wasn't enough. This movie addresses so many issues that African American women face every day. It is not my intention to discuss those issues; that is a different book for another time. Still, every time I watch this movie different points jump out at me depending on what mood I'm in and what is going on in my life at the time. For instance, the scene when Janet Jackson's character reveals to her down low husband that he has given her HIV, and she expresses to him in a melodramatic tone this monologue:

one thing i dont need is any more apologies
i loved you on purpose—i was open on purpose
i cant use another sorry, you're mean/ low-down/
triflin/ & no count straight out
steada bein sorry alla the time enjoy bein yrself

Those words hit me to my heart. It seemed like Ntozake Shange reached into my soul and pulled out every emotion using my blood, sweat and tears to write them on paper. So let's break this poem down. "One thing I don't need is any more apologies" Amen. Aren't you tired of the "I'm sorry's, my apologies, I won't do it again"? I mean really? Please, stop . . . . just stop! If I hear one more I'm sorry or I didn't mean too I think I might lose it! Instead of apologizing again and again, just don't do anything that deserves an apologetic gesture. Like acting right, not cheating, stop lying. I'm just saying. Because I can't use another "sorry," and I definitely don't want another one. Like the poem says, "you're mean, low-down and trifling." Now I could have come up with a few more descriptive words then those, but they will do. This line sums it all up "steada bein sorry alla the time enjoy bein yrself." Sorry, sorry.

My favorite lines of the poem are "I loved you on purpose . . . I was open on purpose." Now, this is my problem. I love the wrong people on purpose. I open myself completely and fully to someone on purpose. I actively participated in every moment of the creation of each relationship. The more confusing part of it all was realizing that the only thing more impossible than staying in the relationship was leaving. How is it that the overanalyzing, compulsive researcher, detailed-oriented person falls in love on purpose with someone who does not deserve to be even liked on purpose? Being open with someone on purpose consists of opening your heart, your soul and your body to them. First mistake: Opening myself to someone other than my husband. Never give yourself or your goodies to someone who has not made a vow and covenant to God and you.

"I Loved you on Purpose" by The Emancipation of Dani's Alex's

I chose to get to know you when I knew enough.
I chose to express my feelings when I should have kept
them to myself.
I chose to believe you when I knew you were lying.
Now, I am choosing to gradually exit your life and never
compromise my morals for the sake of love again.

Lesson Learned: Love is a choice. We choose to love. We choose to accept behaviors we know we should not allow. We choose to participate in a lie for our own selfish gain. We choose to hurt someone else to make ourselves feel better. We choose to follow our heart even when we know its bias. We choose to hurt in hopes of feeling love again.

One thing that I have learned in the midst of all of my drama is to praise under pressure and worship while I'm weeping. My relationship with God became even more real during those dark times when I was mad at God and myself. The times when I felt like He disappointed me, didn't come through and left me alone. Or the times that I fasted, prayed and sacrificed everything I wanted, and He still didn't give me the desires of my heart or even worse became silent. Have you ever been in a relationship with someone and have given them your all, made sacrifices, did everything you thought they wanted and some, and then they become distant? Or better yet silent? Well, that is how God has made me feel on multiple occasions. Those are the times when I revert to all I know. Worship. I was born a worshipper. God distinctively designed every limb of my body and my voice to worship Him. When I'm happy, crying, depressed, confused or feel like giving up. Worship is the one and only thing that brings me through the hardest times. I could choose to do a lot of things in those times, but I choose to worship.

NOTES

CHAPTER

MR. RIGHTFULLY WRONG

When loving you is wrong,
I need to be right

𝒥ust when I thought I made it to level ground, escaped from the enemy and beginning to get my happy back I did the thing that you should never do—let my guard down. Finally, I was in a good place emotionally, though not quite spiritually (but working on that daily). Then walks in this tall, dark, handsome, chocolate brother with dimples. He was educated, intelligent, beautiful smile, wealthy, powerful, status, accomplished, intriguing and born conservationist—all are characteristics that Charles embodied. He was the first man to fill all the checkboxes on "my list." I tell ya, that ol' devil was getting better and better with practice. I mean when I say the bait he was dangling was worth taking the chance of being hooked (pun intended), let's just say this man—and I do mean MAN—had me at hello.

So, it all began one innocent day at the office. My mentor suggested that I meet with this senior executive that worked for the company. As usual, I took her advice and set an appointment with him. A few days later, I walk into Charles' office and was pleasantly surprised that this senior level executive was a brother, a fine brother, a well-dressed brother, who could wear the heck out of a tailor-made, custom-fit suit, and Gucci loafers. Of course, I did not let him see my surprise, immediate approval, or the interest that was building up strongly within. I remained calm, cool, collected and professional and proceeded with the meeting. We talked, he told me about his background, career path, accomplishments and numerous accolades, which were all displayed around his office. That was all fine and well, but my eyes were looking for a wedding band, family pictures, etc. There was nothing to be found. We ended our meeting (an hour and a half past our scheduled allotted time) and went back to work. When I left, I took a moment and rehashed the dialogue between us as well as the interaction. I mean, was I in a fantasy world or did I just experience love at first sight? Either way, I was intrigued and wanted to know about this perfect mystery man. As I do with everyone I meet with, I sent him a thank you email and for some reason got jazzy and said that we should catch a Magic game someday. Send. Really Raevyn? Did I really do that? Yep. Now that could have gone really bad if this man was married; insubordination or just simple rejection from a grown 35-year-old man to a young and overly confident associate. Well, whatever happened was cool with me. I put it out there and that's it. Unfortunately, he did not respond and that was the end. So I thought . . . I did not see him around the building for weeks after or initial meeting. Then I attended a mixer at the office, and he was there. He spoke, worked the room; I did the same and that was it.

Around the holidays some friends came in town and we decided to visit a local lounge. I had never frequented this place, but was excited to get out and have a good time with friends. We pre-gamed at my condo and were on our way. When we get to the lounge, we immediately hit the dance floor. As I was doing my thing, I noticed that Charles was in the building. I was shocked and a little uncomfortable because as a senior vice president of my employer, I didn't want him to have the wrong impression of me. So, I turned to my home girl, told her who he was, and said we should leave and find somewhere else to go. As we were getting everyone together to leave, Charles and I crossed paths. He said something heart melting like "You look breathtaking tonight," and in my tipsy state all I could get out was "likewise." I was very cautious of my words because I was slightly intoxicated and didn't want to be too bold and tell him how I really felt about how good it was to see him and how scrumptious he was looking. I attempted to make the exchange as short as possible, but I noticed that he was slurring a little himself. He seemed to have been having a merry ol' time also. He asked if I would like a drink, but I regretfully declined and said we were just leaving. He said, "You just got here, I saw you when you walked in." Oh, so he was aware when I arrived and seemed like he didn't want me to leave.

I can't recall the transition, but all I can remember is we went from talking, being the only two on the dance floor, to taking shots and making out in a private VIP section. Now, I can honestly say that I have never "made love in the club" with a boyfriend or perfect stranger. But that night, I did and enjoyed every minute of it. We talked, laughed, danced, drank, ate and danced some more. All of the fantasies I conjured up in my head when we initially met were coming true. At the end of the night, the lounge was closing, my friends had already left, his friends left, and it was just he and I, still dancing and not wanting the night to end. We eventually made it to his Range Rover, (my dream car) and he drove me home. When we arrived at my high rise, we sat in the truck talked for hours, kissed for hours, and I finally had to catch my breath and wake up from what seemed to be the best dream ever. We kissed and said goodnight.

As things progressed, we talked on the phone, texted and went on weekly dates. We both were intrigued and challenged by the other. We thrived off of the adrenaline of sneaking around the office, yet mesmerized by the instant chemistry that intensified every time we were together. I had never experienced feelings of this magnitude before. It wasn't only lust because I knew that feeling all too well. It wasn't purely love. The only way I could describe it would be extreme passion.

As we continued to date, I began to see red flags, but I chose to ignore them. I was enjoying his company, the benefits of being with him and the passion he so expertly gave me. There were multiple occasions when his friend would reference someone else as if I was aware of another woman. When I would question his friend he would begin to change his statements. After all, he was a lawyer and knew exactly how to utilize his words in the best interest of Charles. When the high of Charles began to dwindle and I had the choice to get another hit or face reality, I began asking questions. I asked if he was married, engaged, in a relationship, or did he have someone in waiting? His answer was always no. He would assure me that I was the only woman in his life. Now, I could have continued to inquire to get to the truth, but let me keep it real: I didn't really want the truth. If being with him was wrong, I didn't want to be right. So, we continued to date. He would tell me he loved me and our time together was magical.

Eventually, I began to consider relocating. I didn't want to leave him, but I knew it was time to begin a new chapter of my life. I asked him what did he think about me moving and he said he didn't want me to leave, but he wanted me to make the best decision for me. All I wanted him to do was to ask me to stay. We discussed the state of our relationship and what the future held for our long-distance relationship, and we committed to making it work. I knew deep down inside that I if I left it was over.

Leaving was one of the hardest decisions I have ever had to make. If I stayed, I was sure the truth would eventually come out about him, and I would be devastated. If I left, I was walking away from my fantasy. It's no fun when you love someone but can't be with them because they are not the right one for you.

When the day came to leave, I was an emotional wreck. I couldn't pack or even tell the movers what to pack. It was a bittersweet moment. I was leaving Charles for Atlanta, leaving my dream man for my dream city. As difficult as it was it took the help of my mom and brother to help me not to change my mind. It seemed like a scene taken from a movie, in slow motion with sad music playing in the background as Charles came to my condo just as I was about to leave. We hugged and kissed in the rain. He said he loved me and would call me while I was on the road.

While driving to Atlanta, I contemplated turning around each mile that went by. When my mom, brother, and I reached Atlanta, I was numb. I knew that I was where I wanted to be, but I also knew my relationship with Charles was over. As the days and weeks went by, he would call, we would chat, and we would plan trips to see each other that never happened.

One weekend, the same mentor that introduced us came into town. I picked her up from the airport, and we went to dinner. In the midst of our conversation she said, "Charles proposed to that girl!" "What?!? What girl?" I asked. As I strained to not throw up all of my food while not showing her my surprise, hurt and anger, since she did not know about our relationship, as we all worked for the same company. She said the girl he has been with for some time now. She said she only met her on a few business occasions. I couldn't get myself together for the rest of the evening. I dropped her off at her hotel and cried as I drove home. Something told me to Google the both of their names, and what pops up? Their wedding website. Live and in color, photos of the two of them, and one of "our" songs playing in the background. I just couldn't believe my eyes. I read about the proposal, which took place months before I moved and while we were together. This was all too much to take in. This ninja was playing me all along. From the information on the site, they had been dating for years.

All the red flags and comments from his friend made perfect sense. Was I hurt? Yes. Was I even more embarrassed that I had been played? Heck yeah! Did I regret being with him? Not one bit. I just added him to my most favorite mistakes list.

My first thought was to call him and go completely off on him, but I didn't. Instead, I wanted to see when or if he was ever going to tell me. Thanks to the site I knew that his engagement party was coming up, so when he called I told him that I was planning to come visit him that same weekend. This fool was still playing games and told me to come. Of course I didn't go and he calls me the night of his engagement party saying how much he missed me and thought I was coming in town. Apparently, I was quickly falling into the role of side chick, and that once he got married he was going to promote me to mistress. Ha!

When I realized he was never going to admit any form of the truth. I stopped answering his calls and text messages and moved on with my life. Thank God I did not choose him over me.

Lessons Learned: Always choose you. Never allow someone to place you in a role that goes against your beliefs and standards. If a man will cheat on his significant other with you, then he will cheat on you with someone of even less significance. If you choose to ignore the red flags and live in your fantasy, be prepared for the nightmare when you wake up. Most importantly, if it seems too good to be true, it probably is.

INSULTING MY INTELLIGENCE

My number one pet peeve in a relationship or friendship is a bad liar. If you see the need to lie to me, at least make it believable and not get caught up in it. Some people just lie for no reason. Some voluntarily lie, and others lie when asked the right questions. As a disclaimer, when I'm getting to know someone, I let them know that if they are going to lie to me then they better be on point and not let me catch them in the lie.

In most cases, if I ask you a direct question then I probably already know something is up or have a strong inclination that something is not right. My definition of lying is a direct insult to my intelligence. Lying by omission is a form of lying, too. Now I can admit that I fall into this category sometimes. I won't outright lie if you ask the right question, but if you don't then I won't tell the truth either. Probably not the right thing to do, but anyone that knows me knows to ask specific questions and I will give you specific truthful answers. It's funny how life experiences dictate how we react to certain situations.

My first love, Ray, was a pathological, expert liar. He would lie so good that I thought I was the one crazy. I mean really, I could see something with my own eyes, and he would conjure up a story so good that I would question what I saw. SMH, this ninja could lie his way out of any and everything. He taught me how to lie. I was young, naïve and green. It took me a few years to catch on, but when I did I was tainted and paranoid. I believed everyone was a liar. Guilty until proven innocent. Like my bestie and me would always say, "Trust then verify."

Then there was Charles—now he was the best liar I have ever dealt with. Now when I say that my pet peeve is a bad liar, he is the epitome of a professional liar. We dated for almost a year, and for some stupid reason I chose to trust him until he gave me a reason not to, and this ninja tried my life. His lies were well spoken, articulate, calculated and smooth. I know women who are so into a man that they choose to believe his lies even though they know the truth. Well, that was not the case with him. I always had an inclination that this man was too good to be true, and in his case he definitely was. I would ask him direct questions like is there someone else? Ex-girlfriend? Fiancée? Wife? He would respond with a direct, "No, Raevyn, I love you" while looking me straight in my eyes. The signs of someone lying to you were not there. He didn't look to the left, shrug his shoulder, or wrinkle his forehead. I knew something wasn't right, and there was a lot that he wasn't telling me, but I just went with it. Good things don't end, unless they end badly.

All the red flags were there. My woman's sixth sense was in full effect, and like an idiot I tried to suppress it. In the end, this ninja was engaged, and his fiancée lived with him. To make it plain, I got played.

FIRST IN THE NATURAL, THEN IN THE SPIRITUAL

If something happened to the car, house or health, my mom would always use the phrase "first in the natural, then in the spiritual," meaning, there is some spiritual significance to the occurrences that are happening. For example, when the suspension fault light came on in my four-month-old Range Rover, my first reaction was to be alarmed and slightly frustrated. I just bought this truck, and there is a problem already?! First, I told myself to calm down and figure out what's going on. Land Rovers are made for off-road and mountain driving, so the manufacturer equips the truck with different settings such as, highway, mountains, desert and unleveled plains. I read the manual to see what the light was indicating. It read, "If the light flashes red, a serious suspension fault has been detected and the vehicle should be driven carefully until qualified assistance can be obtained."

My next thoughts were, "It is always something! I just can't win for losing." I wondered how much the repairs were going to cost. As I continued to drive and look at the light on my dashboard, I noticed that it is a truck with two arrows on each side, portraying the vehicle to be imbalanced, not stable. Then I looked up the definition of suspension; Webster defines it as: 1. *The action of suspending someone or something or the condition of being suspended, in particular. 2. The temporary prevention of something from continuing or being in force or effect.* Which caused me to look up the word suspend or suspended which means *1. To bar for a period from a privilege, office, or position, usually as a punishment; 2. To cause to stop for a period; interrupt; 3. a.*

*To hold in abeyance; defer; **b.** To render temporarily ineffective;* ***4.*** *To hang so as to allow free movement;* ***5.*** *To support or keep from falling without apparent attachment, as by buoyancy;* ***1.*** *To cease for a period; delay;* ***2.*** *To fail to make payments or meet obligations.*

After reading the definitions, all I could say was, "I hear you God." During this time, I was going through a weird time in my life. It seemed like nothing was going the way I wanted it to go and I was simply existing without a purpose. I had been unproductive, discontent and overwhelmed with feelings of despair. I had been asking God what was going on. What was my life coming to? In that moment, God spoke to me and said, "You have been spiritually suspended due to your disobedience." He had me in a place of suspension between opposition and opportunity. Due to my disobedience, God had prevented me from continuing to be comfortable with the life He had so graciously blessed me with. My discontentment was Him suspending me from my privileges of being a child of the King. I had officially been placed on a spiritual punishment. My whole life had been interrupted, placed on pause, suspended. I was temporarily ineffective, and I felt miserable. All of the pain and discomfort that I had been praying and crying about was all caused by the one and only. My emotions and the essence of my being was experiencing just what my truck was experiencing—a bumpy, hard and wavering ride. Not being able to adjust to the terrains of life, adjusting up, down, side to side. God equipped us to withstand any terrain that we will come across on this road called life. Whether it is a mountain high, valley low, desert sand or winters snow. We are designed to operate and perform through it all. Not having the capability to properly align with the will of God. There was a system (spiritual) fault, I was imbalanced and unleveled, not functioning in the proper way that God designed for me to operate.

Another situation was with my BMW. I don't know why all of my revelations and epiphany's relate to my vehicles, but hey whatever it takes for God to get His point across, I'll take it. As I was saying, I was driving to Jacksonville to visit my mom. Less than thirty minutes on the road, I get a flat tire. Well, let me be honest and tell the full story. My tire pressure light had been on for a while, but I just ignored it. Now, I am on the side of the road with a flat tire and no spare. Some genius came up with the idea to design run flat tires. These tires go flat, and you have up to 50 miles before you can't drive on them or something like that. Well, it was obvious that I had driven my 50 plus miles and couldn't go any farther. Sitting on the side of the road waiting for a tow truck, I realized how important it is to adhere to the warning signs and caution lights. If I would have had my tires checked when the light came on, all of this could have been avoided. To make the situation even worse, I get the tire repaired, and the tire pressure light was still on. The mechanic told me that the light would remain on because all of the tire sensors were missing. Smh, if it ain't one thing it's another.

Now let's look at this in the spiritual. First, not adhering to the warning light. How many times have you seen red flags in a situation and chose to ignore them? Once the situation has ended badly and caused unnecessary hurt, pain and inconvenience, you say to yourself, "I should have paid attention to the warning." Next, there's tire pressure light and the tire going flat. There were external and internal pressures in my life that were literally sucking the air out of me slowly and causing me to become flat. During that time, I was involved with Charles and "running flat" as each day passed by. Which leads me to my last lesson learned, the tire sensors missing. The sensors are designed to monitor the air pressure in the tires and alert the driver if the air pressure goes above or below the specified pressure level. The purpose of the sensors is to maintain pressure levels in the tires to allow the vehicle to be balanced. I'm not going to say that Charles pressured me into doing anything that I did not already want to do. However, I do believe that I was imbalanced and running flat spiritually without the capability of moving forward. Basically, I was sitting on the side of the road waiting for a pick me up.

I view our spiritual conscious as our dashboard. It always lets you know when something is wrong. We have the ability to keep riding along until we break down or go to the dealership and have a diagnostic test to reveal the issues and get them repaired. The diagnostic test gives the mechanic codes that indicate the issues and where they are located but does not tell you the cause. The mechanic has to then use the information provided then go to the location of the issue to see what caused the problem and what needs to be done to repair it. God allows a situation to happen in our lives to cause a light to go off to lead us to Him the ultimate mechanic. He then diagnoses us and tells us what the problem is, where it is located and goes right to that underlining issue and lets us know what needs to be repaired. Isn't God good? He will never let us ride around in life not knowing that we have a problem and breakdown. He gives us a warning light to let us know that something needs to be checked out ASAP. Don't ignore the warning lights, get checked out.

NOTES

CHAPTER

OZ

Not that I speak in respect of want: for I have learned,
in whatsoever state I am, therewith to be content.
Philippians 4:11

I laugh when I think about how badly I wanted to live in Atlanta, almost like it was Oz or something. It's funny to think that I really believed that if I could just get there everything would be great. I'm not sure what I thought was there, I just loved the city and it was my dream to live there. While I was living in Tampa, a friend of mine once said, "Rae, you have everything you want in ATL, here in Tampa." When I thought about what she said, she was absolutely right. I had the corporate America job, the bachelorette high-rise condo overlooking downtown, the luxury vehicle, the well-educated, gainfully employed, Tampa's most eligible bachelor boyfriend, international ministry church that I loved and had the opportunity to serve as a media personality and awesome friends! I really did have it all, but all was in Tampa. I would have done anything to pick up my whole life in Tampa and place it in the heart of Atlanta.

Now that I have had the opportunity to live in my dream city with all of the bells and whistles, God allowed me to see that Oz was not anything special. It was a regular city, with regular people and regular problems.

Lesson Learned: There is no city in the world that can ever give you peace, contentment, joy, completeness or whatever you are in search of. That place can only be found in the will of God.

Not that I speak in respect of want: for I have learned,
in whatsoever state I am, therewith to be content.
Philippians 4:11

COMMON DENOMINATOR

Most people believe that if I could just move to this place then all of your problems will disappear. Not true! I have had so many conversations with people and even been in this exact situation myself thinking that if I could just tap my heels together three times and wish myself to the place I want to be everything else will be perfect. Sometimes it seems like the place we are in is the problem, when really it is the place we are in that is the problem (literally). Regardless where you go, where you live or where you run away to escape. The problem, the issue and YOU will be right there with you. My belief is you take you with you. That philosophy remains the same with geographical relocation for the wrong reasons and even relationships. I have had the opportunity to live all over the United States—Florida, New York, Cincinnati, Connecticut, and Atlanta to name a few. Every place I have lived, the one thing that I always had to pack was Raevyn. I was the common denominator. While I was packing clothes, shoes and furniture, I also had to pack my insecurities, frustrations, emotions and issues.

Do people really believe that the city they are trying to get to is the pot of gold at the end of the rainbow? Obviously. I believed that about Atlanta. Since college, I always wanted to live in Atlanta, not because I was running away from anything or someone, just because I believed that once I made it there everything I ever wanted would follow. Now that I have been living in Atlanta for almost a year, I am so over it! Who would have thought? I have a great job, single and the city at my fingertips. Atlanta has fabulous nightlife, prominent social circles, money, wealthy men, etc. When

I approached my one-year anniversary, I was not impressed nor did I have the desire to remain in Atlanta. Oddly enough, I did not go out, had not made any real friends, had not found a church, and most importantly my husband had not found me! Hotlanta was not so hot.

Lesson Learned: You take YOU with you. No matter what city you are in or what city you want to be in, you are the common denominator. Changing your location does not change your situation. The place we all should desire to be and run to is God's will. God's will is the place where our issues will be resolved, problems put to rest, and the true pot of gold can be found at the end of the rainbow.

NOTES

_____

_____

_____

_____

_____

CHAPTER

I'M HAPPY FOR YOU, BUT I'M HURTING FOR ME

"A woman's heart should be so hidden in Christ that a man has to seek Him first to find her."

Have you ever wanted something so bad and it seemed like no matter what you did, it wouldn't happen? Well, that seems to be the story of my life. All I have ever wanted was to be happily married, have a family, and a successful career while fulfilling my purpose and destiny in life. That's all. Sounds like a lot, huh? I don't think it is, however it seems like God all of a sudden is having a hard time fulfilling my request. I am trying my best not to resent God and his plan, but it's hard when everyone around me is getting what *I* want.

For instance, my best friend—she was always the tomboy, anti-girly girl who never really expressed the desire to get married young and start a family—is married, living in Georgia, and has my beautiful goddaughter. It's not that I'm not happy for her because I am, but I am just hurting for me. I would give anything to be in her shoes (so I think). I try to make myself feel better by saying that I really wouldn't want her exact situation because would I really want to give up my MBA, financial security, freedom to travel all around the world, my prestigious corporate America job, one-bedroom, high-rise luxury condo, BMW, regular shopping sprees and fabulous lifestyle? Honestly, no. I want it ALL! My bff has given up a lot, missed out on opportunities and experiences that I've been blessed and fortunate enough to have. I wouldn't trade the life that I have been blessed with and definitely not worthy of, but there is a void in my life that makes me want to give it all up for what I think I want. Some people say that the grass is always greener on the other side and there are times when we want what we cannot have and that statement is true. I pose the question of am I willing to pay the high water bill to keep my grass greener?

Right now, I am at a place in my life when I have everything I need just not everything I want.

NEXT IN LINE

One thing I have learned about myself is that I am never comfortable with my current state. I am always wanting more, always reaching for something higher. Now I wonder, "Where do I go from here?" My life is imbalanced. I long for a true relationship. I desire to have a partner to join me on this journey called life, someone I can talk to, express how I feel, tell my inner emotions and not feel like an added burden. Someone who knows me well inside and out and who is spiritually connected to me. It's not about a physical attraction, but a spiritual attraction. I want someone who is the perfect match for my soul. A true soul mate. I have had the "perfect man," the man who could check off everybody box on "my list" and when I got exactly what I wanted it was not what I needed. While in that situation—at this point, I can't even refer to it as a relationship—I was happy and miserable at the same time. Some women would have died for that opportunity and thought I was crazy when I let it go, but why would I stay in something that ultimately I knew wasn't right for me? Yes, I have made many mistakes. But none of them I regret because I always follow my heart and do what makes me happy. I have never been the type of person to think about what other people say or think. I'm a firm believer that you have to do you and follow your gut. No one knows what's best for you but you and God.

I have never been the jealous type, wanting what someone else has or his or her life. But observing my friend's life from the outside, I do want my dream, my happily ever after. I am extremely ecstatic for everyone who has found true love, engagement, marriage and family. I am happy for them; I am just hurting for me. I keep saying that I am patiently waiting, but when is God going to send my husband? His Word tells us that He did not make it for man to be alone, and throughout the Bible he always did things in two. So why am I alone? God has not revealed that answer to me, but what I know for sure is that I refuse to move ahead of Him and I refuse to settle for less than His best! God has great things in store for me, and I don't mind waiting on the Lord.

Lesson Learned: When you're experiencing feelings of loneliness, listen to the still small voice telling you to be strong because sometimes struggle is God's will. Even when you feel delayed and you do not understand the struggle, just know that God is always on time. Though the pressures of life seems to weigh you down and you don't know which way to turn, God is concerned and He's working it out for you. Get ready for your miracle, move to the front of the line. Today is your day. You're next in line for a miracle.

LIVING SINGLE

God have you really called me to a life of singleness? I mean, really? Will I live the rest of my life alone? No one to love, without a lifelong partner, a husband to have a family with? As the holidays approach, I wish I had a family to cook Thanksgiving dinner for, to take family portraits for Christmas cards, and someone to bring the New Year in with a kiss. I do not need someone to complete me, I am a whole person. However, it would be nice to have someone to become "one" with. I'm just saying God, you did not create man to live alone, no man is an island, right? So where is my Boaz, Adam, my MAN???

The more I ponder the thoughts of why God has not given me my No. 1 desire of marriage and relationship, He begins to low key go off on me, reminding me of the many prophesies He has given instructing me that there are specific things He wants me to accomplish while I am yet single. Once I have fulfilled those things and have completely delighted myself in Him, then and only then He would allow my husband to find me. My husband will find me doing the work of the Kingdom. I politely interrupted Him by saying, "I know, I know, BUT is there any way you can send Him now and I promise to still fulfill the purpose You have for me?" He simply replied, "You prayed for my perfect will to be done in your life and this is how it has to be." There was nothing left for me to say. This is when the stubborn part of me fights so hard. I want God's perfect will AND Raevyn's "perfect" will. Or in this case, I am willing to settle for His permissible will. His perfect will just seems to be impossible, farfetched and extremely hard to reach. What's a girl to do? These are the times when He is a keeper. Right this minute, God is keeping me and I do not want to be kept. I would rather give up, do things on my own and make it happen for myself. Ecclesiastes 3:11 says, "He hath made every thing beautiful in his time: also he hath set the world in their heart, so that no man can find out the work that God maketh from the beginning to the end." As hard as it is, I have to be patient and obedient.

Lesson Learned: There are things in your life that God has promised and other things you desire. Just know that if God promised it, He will keep His promise. Don't get so caught up in what you want and when you want it like me. Be patient and know that everything will be made beautiful in its time, God's time.

"A woman's heart should be so hidden in Christ that a
man has to seek Him first to find her."

NOTES

_____

_____

_____

_____

_____

_____

CHAPTER

11

REAL-ATIONSHIPS

"And the Lord, he it is that doth go before thee; he will be with thee, he will not fail thee, neither forsake thee: fear not, neither be dismayed."

Deuteronomy 31:8

Have you ever had a moment where you thought about how life has played itself out so far? I recently had that moment. For some reason, I was led to catch up on the lives of my past friends. One just got married and another one is engaged. As I browse through their photos, I see how happy everyone seems and think to myself, "People have really moved on with their lives." Things are different and are continuing to change. As I click to the next picture, I became sad, discontent and somewhat uncomfortable with where my life is currently and how it is going. I never thought that I would be 24, in the city I love, a great job, lonely and discontent. I do not want to sound ungrateful or like I'm complaining because I thank God for all of His many blessings. However, life was just not the way I pictured or planned for it to be. I don't know if God has me in this place for a season or reason, but I wish I knew what this process was all about. Maybe if I understood what He is trying to do, then just maybe it would make things a little easier.

I sat in the dark, on a Friday night, alone, in Atlanta. That had been the story of my life for a while now. I was completely fulfilled in my professional life and completely depleted in my personal life. My personal life was non-existent. How did I get to that place? What did I do? Where did things change? I noticed the things I had control over were great in my life: my job, my location, and my money. But the things that I did not control were simply out of control. Relationships are things that I cannot control because other people are involved.

My family relationships have dwindled. In the past, I have always been a family-oriented person. My mommy, Granny, Auntie La La and Uncle Tony always have been my support system, my spiritual counsel, personal board of directors, and most importantly my friends. They were the people I could go to about anything without being judged, looked down upon, or criticized. I knew without a shout of a doubt that they did not have any hidden agendas or motives and had my best interest at heart. Somewhere down the road I chose to terminate my BOD. Why? In response to some situations that have transpired over the past few years and I have cut off some of the closest people to me—my family, friends and people who genuinely cared for me. I keep asking myself why I went down this road of exclusion. Why have I chosen to end life-long relationships and friendships and put a guard up to the people who love me? In this new life that I am in, I am surrounded everyday by acquaintances, associates, colleagues and so-called friends. None of these people know me, the real Raevyn. I am just passing through their lives; I know that our "relationships" are going to be only for a season. I miss my friends, my sisters, the girls—now women—that I grew up with, laughed with, cried with, fought with and made-up with. The memories we shared are priceless. I feel like I'm missing out on all the memories we dreamed about and planned when we were younger. There are a lot of things you can get back, but when time and memories are gone, they are gone forever. How do I make things right? Is there a way to change things? How can I control things that are out of my control? My family and friends did not walk out of my life, I'm the one who disappeared and disconnected, for no real reason at all.

At first, I felt like God had hidden me away for a season to help prepare me for things to come. But now I feel like I'm in exile. My greatest fear in life is to live a life without purpose, not be in the will of God and to never fulfill the great destiny that God has placed on my life. Some of my other fears are living my life with the wrong person or spending the rest of my life alone. I do not want to be that super successful, wealthy, SINGLE mogul, having all the money, big house, luxury cars and having no one to enjoy it with. There are so many women who have it all in all aspects of their lives yet are lacking emotionally and relationally. I WANT IT ALL! I want to be wealthy materially, spiritually and emotionally. Then I ask myself, is it possible to actually have it all? I don't know if it is, but I do not mind trying until I figure it out. I have never really voiced these feelings to anyone because I do not want to sound ungrateful or come off like I am complaining because most people really just do not understand. They look at my life, credentials, accomplishments and accolades and say I have it all. They just cease to understand my inner struggle. No one can relate to the sacrifices I have made and the discipline needed to be where I am today. It may look glamorous and sexy on the outside, but can you see the nights I have cried myself to sleep with overwhelming emotions of loneliness, rejection and disappointment? Can you see the instability of living in more than three states in one year— packing up your life, moving to a city by yourself, knowing no one and as soon as you get settled your up and moving again? No one knows the warfare and intense battles I face every day in my profession striving for a spirit of excellence, having to prove myself to the tenth power just to be equal, fighting racist spirits and people feeling intimidated by me for no reason.

I have worked all over the United States and in the past year I've worked in Cincinnati, Tampa, and Atlanta. Working in Cincy was a culture shock to say the least. I was working in the one of the most conservative, male-dominated, Caucasian banks. I am usually good at adapting to my surroundings, but when you are fleeting a spiritual fight and end up going directly into another one, you run out of strength and get tired. Tampa was a different situation in itself, and you would think Atlanta would be a bit easier due to its large African American population, but I have found it to be even harder. It seems as if the executives in my company are not accustomed to educated, articulate, intelligent, young African American women, which makes me have to overexert myself and be sure to not mess up because they are looking for any reason to disqualify me. Always know that looks are deceiving. Don't be fooled by how things look on the outside. Never covet someone else's position or lifestyle because you have no clue what it took to get them there and keep them there. And by my own experience, I know that everything that glitters ain't gold and everything that sparkles ain't diamonds.

Raevyn

INSIDE OUT

For the past few months, maybe even longer I have been going through spiritual augmentation—"spiritual surgery"—which is the same thing as plastic surgery, just on the inside. The society we live in today is as superficial and plastic as Barbie and Ken. If a woman doesn't like her breasts, she gets breast implants; if she wants fuller lips, she gets lip injections, and the new thing now is butt pads and butt injections. This epidemic is causing people to be beautiful on the outside (some of them and others not so much) but mutilated on the inside. If I was to be completely honest with myself, I was that person. Pretending as if everything was perfect in my world, but on the inside I was miserable and unhappy. I didn't need plastic surgery, what I needed was spiritual surgery. I needed the ultimate doctor to go in and uplift my soul out of the miry clay, inject my purpose with passion and suck out the despair that had me hopeless. I carry the burden for my generation, the generation of quick fixes, unrealistic images and expensive facades. The world is beginning to make it seem easy to change the things you do not like about your outward appearance, but does that change who you are? Does it magically remove your insecurities? No it doesn't. It is just an expensive way to mask the issues you have inside.

Lesson Learned for the Ladies: God has created you in His image. Everything He made, including you, is good. Accept your thick thighs, flat or voluptuous breasts, round derriere or the lack there of. Just be who you are, the person God specifically created and designed you to be. There is no one that looks like you. He purposefully did not make any two people just alike, not even twins. So why change your physical features to look like someone else? If you want to change something, change the world! Change your mindset! Change those ugly things that you are holding on to inside. You are beautiful. You possess the "Beauty of Holiness".

SOLITARY CONFINEMENT

The one thing that has always been unbreakable and consistent is the bond between my family and me. Since I was born I have had a close relationship with my mommy, granny, granddaddy, Auntie La La, Uncle Tony and great-grandmother. They were my support system, spiritual counselors, and confidants and in some seasons my best friends. They were the people who I always knew I could count on and depend on through thick and thin. Even through some of those hard times they interceded on my behalf, showed me tough love and was always there when I needed to vent or just a shoulder to cry on. Family is something that God blesses us with knowing exactly the kind of people we are going to need as we go through life. We don't choose our family. They are pre-chosen specifically for us.

Over the years I have come to accept the family that God has placed me in. At one point, I resented my family and was estranged from them for a while. They never did anything to intentionally hurt me, but the devil tricked me into thinking that I did not need them and they were not on my side, when in all actuality, they were the only ones on my side. I prayed that our relationships would be restored in God's timing. God granted my prayer and blessed us to be closer than before.

REJECTION IS GOD'S PROTECTION

Daddy/daughter issues. The relationship between a father and daughter is a complex one. Surprisingly, this dynamic is explored less than other relationships. A girl's relationship with her father is a direct representation of her personal life. A little girl's first interaction and relationship with the opposite sex is with that of her father. Whether the father is active in her life or whether he is an absent father, his role is vital to her emotional development.

When I was born, my father was physically abusive to my mother, an alcoholic, cheater, hormonally imbalanced, and an inexperienced father. He was young, never had been a father before, and though his father was always in his life he was not the best example of a godly father. I do not recall most of my infant and toddler years, but from photos he was always there for birthdays, trips to Disney World and family functions. Looking back, I do remember him being present to celebrate the holidays and milestone moments, but I cannot remember ever developing an emotional connection or relationship with him. As a baby, I always knew him as my father but never as my daddy. I believe there is a difference between being a father and being a daddy. To me, a father is a man who biologically assisted in my conception. A daddy is a man who loving assisted in my development into a woman. My parents divorced when I was five or six years old. My mom always tried to encourage a relationship with my father until I was older and could make the choice for myself. He would send birthday cards and gifts each year, and on some occasions pick me up to visit my grandparents. In reality, he was a stranger to me. I didn't know much about him because he was always a private person (which is where I get my need of privacy from).

As I grew older and developed a relationship with Christ for myself, I began to feel a void in my life. Being young and unable to process my feelings of incompleteness, I began to fill that void with the wrong thing: Boys. My maternal grandfather, who I affectionately called "Daddy," was indeed my daddy. He was the man who loved me, protected me and introduced me to male/female interaction since the day I was born. God loved me so much that he allowed me the opportunity to grow up with a father figure who covered my mommy and me until God called him home.

At a young age, I experienced a form of rejection. Unknown to me as a toddler, my father rejected me. His rejection was not intentional; it was due to lack of knowledge and not knowing how to be vulnerable to an innocent baby girl. Over time, a surface level relationship was built but nothing of substance. Nothing that would mend the wounds of a little girl being left to face the world uncovered by her father. As I grew older, I began to hate my father for not being there. I felt like I would not have gotten into the bad relationships, became sexually active at such a young age, and have experienced so much heartbreak if he would had just been there to protect me from the boys, the men, the liars, the cheaters, everything! I was young and naïve and looking for love in all the wrong places. My mommy did the best she could, but there are some areas in life that only a father's love can help ease the pain.

During this time, God revealed to me that He was my father and would never leave me nor forsake me. Those words have comforted me all my life. I've learned that sometimes rejection is God's protection. God knew who my father would be and the issues he would have. He also knew that my father's strength, analytical intelligence, logic and reasoning abilities, athleticism, and strategic mindset were all characteristics that I would inherit. God had a master plan when he orchestrated for the DNA of my father and mother to perfectly come together to create me. He was equipping me with all of the tools I needed. I may not have had the fairy tale daddy's girl story, but I will never know the things God was protecting me from.

There are times I still battle with feelings of rejection and unfulfilled voids. The Lord reassures me that *"And the Lord, he it is that doth go before thee; he will be with thee, he will not fail thee, neither forsake thee: fear not, neither be dismayed."* *Deuteronomy 31:8*

Lesson Learned: There is no love like the *real* Father's love. He always will be with you to guide and protect you. My earthly father did the best he could. I no longer hold feelings of anger or resentment toward him. Surprisingly, I am thankful for him. He may not have been there when I wanted him to be, but I thank him for being there for me in the times I needed him to be. He was not the perfect father, and I was not the perfect daughter. Coincidentally, the same goes for my relationship with Christ. They both still love me unconditionally. Every day I strive to be a better Christian and daughter and strive to fulfill God's commandment: *"Children, obey your parents in the Lord, for this is right. 2 Honour thy father and mother; which is the first commandment with promise; 3 That it may be well with thee, and thoumayest live long on the earth." Ephesian 6:1-3*

Allow God the opportunity to heal your deepest hurts and pain. He is the only person who can fill your voids of rejection, abandonment and betrayal. Do not let your pain make you bitter; instead, allow it to make you better. Stop holding on to what happened to you, who wasn't there, or what they did to you. You are a survivor. You are still here. It didn't kill you . . . it *made* you.

NOTES

_____

_____

_____

_____

_____

_____

_____

_____

_____

_____

LOVE THE PERSON YOU'RE WITH

ASK, BELIEVE, RECEIVE.

One of the hardest things to do in life is to accept the fact that you cannot be with the person you want to be with. There is a saying, "If you're not with the person you love, then love the person you are with." Is this actually possible? How can I love the person I am with when I am in love with someone else? My granny use to tell me, "be with the person who loves me the most, not the person I love the most." I always bucked that advice, and when I would question her, her response would always be "You can learn to love them." Back then, her advice and words of wisdom made absolutely no sense to me whatsoever. I wanted to be with the person I loved the most. I didn't want to have to learn to love them all I wanted to learn was how to express my love for them even more.

When people say that hindsight is always 20/20, I cannot help but to agree. Most of the relationships that I have discussed in this book were all products of me loving someone more than they loved me. And you see what happened to those relationships: epic fail. There is something about a man loving his significant other more than he thinks she loves him. It all goes back to "the chase." Men like to chase and conquer their prey (aka women). If we are helplessly and desperately in love with them, there is nothing for them to conquer. That is when men give up and go on to the next woman before we know it. My mom once gave me a good visual to explain this. My stepdad likes to hunt deer. When he goes hunting, he and the guys stake out their deer and strategically and quietly go after it. Now you have two types of deer. You have the ones that are slow, out in the open, and easy to kill. Then you have the ones that are fast, hiding, and a challenge to kill. Which deer do you think the men go after? Not the one that is prancing around and an easy target. They go after the deer that is the hardest to kill, the one that they spend all day and night chasing after and trying to conquer. That's the one they want, and the one that means the most to them. The same thing goes for relationships and dating. Men do not want the easy women; they want the woman who is going to challenge them and make them chase her. Now, I'm sure some men will disagree with my philosophy and that's cool. You try it for yourself. Be quick, fast and uncatchable and see what types of hoops men will jump through to catch you. Once he catches you, you won't have to worry about him going hunting again.

YOU DON'T COMPLETE ME

I complete him. What do you do when you are the complete package and you fall in love with someone who is complete baggage? It is one of those situations when you know you are good for him, but he is not good for you. Is it one of situations where opposites attract? Let's say it is. Now what? Is there a way to make someone good for you or are you just placed in their life to make them better and move on to the next project? I have had to deal with similar situations, and I still have not figured out how to deal with this and not be the one hurt in the end. I find myself building up these men, helping them to realize and walk into their callings and becoming the men that God wants them to be, and when my project is complete they move on to be wonderful boyfriends and husbands to someone else. Take Joe for example. I spoke into his life time after time, which influenced him to rededicate his life to Christ, and now he is a Pastor. Ray gave his life to Christ while we were dating, and I believe that he is now in heaven. My second fiancée gave his life to Christ while we were dating in college. God used our relationships to save these men souls.

My mom once told me that this may be my ministry: speaking to the king in these men and calling out what has always been there. That's fine and all, but when is my king going to find me? Is all my work in vain? The more I begin to see God's plan unfold, the less frustration I have and the more anticipation I begin to feel. God has allowed me to be a part of wonderful relationships and a chapter in the story of great men's lives. I know that my future husband is going to be a mighty man of valor, and I will be prepared to be his queen.

Lesson Learned: Learn to love what is good for you.

SAVE FACE

In relationships, we have all been guilty of going through our mate's phone, text messages, email, car, Facebook, Twitter and every other social media account they have. Some say this is a form of insecurity, a lack of trust, or simply looking for proof or evidence of an inclination we may have had. I admit I have had my days of being an undercover "Law & Order" detective or FBI agent. One of those days, I was conducting a criminal investigation and got caught red-handed. When the criminal—I mean my boyfriend—at the time caught me, there was nothing I could say to justify my actions. All he could say was why did you have to go behind my back and sneak to go through my things. All you had to do was ask, and I would have shown you anything you wanted to see (yeah right, you say that now). He continued to say, but instead you wanted to save face and go behind my back.

Even though he should have been the one in the wrong, I was the one arrested with conviction and guilt. Why is it that I wanted to save face and not come clean that I was experiencing feelings of insecurity or paranoia about our relationship? There is a myth that when someone is wrongfully accuses you of cheating or unfaithfulness it is because they are guilty of a similar action.

Lesson Learned: Be honest about your vulnerabilities. They are not a weakness; they are areas of improvement and healing.

If you are in a relationship, and you want to find out something, just ask. If that's not good enough, be bold enough to investigate in the open when the other person is present. There is no need to "save face" with someone you profess to love. Create a safe environment of trust and honesty in your relationship. If you can't be your authentic self with your mate, then who can you be yourself with?

FEAR

Lately, I have observed the relationships and marriages around me. To be honest, it is almost depressing and discouraging. It seems like no one is happily married. I understand that life or marriage is not a bed of roses, but dang, is it even bearable?

My perception, the reality, and my dream of marriage are all completely different. Being a product of an abusive marriage and

divorce, growing up in my mom's second marriage that has had its share of issues, and most recently observing newlyweds with my best friend's marriage, on all these levels, one thing about marriage that remains constant is the fact that it is hard. Having the advantage of using other couple's marriage as real life experience for me has been beneficial and detrimental to my outlook. My personal diagnosis of my view on marriage is that I have the desire to be happily married. Doesn't everyone? I do not have a fear of commitment or marriage, but a fear of settling or struggling unnecessarily within the confines of marriage. My best friend once said during a rough time in her marriage that, she felt like she messed up by trying to do the right thing. She got married because she was committing sexual sin, so she and husband wanted to do the honorable thing and get married. Better to marry than to burn. But her comment really stuck with me. How is it that you feel like after making such a serious commitment to God and another person that you messed up trying to do the right thing? I would think that God would honor their desire to please Him and do the right thing by blessing their marriage and not making it so hard.

Sometimes women call themselves doing the right thing, but do not consult with God about what is His right thing for them and their lives. That is where I am now. I live a comfortable single life. God has been my father and husband. I hope and pray that when it's time for me to do the right thing, it is exactly that . . . the right thing.

IT'S NOT YOU, IT'S ME

Regardless where you go, what you do or who you are in a relationship with . . . YOU are the common denominator. After failed relationship after failed relationship, I began to wonder why every guy I thought was "the one" was the one who hurt and disappointed me yet again. It seemed like I had a pattern of dating the same uneducated, career lacking, financially unsecure, personal improvement project person just with a different name. What attracted me to these men? Why couldn't I be attracted to a godly, wealthy, successful, driven man who treated me like a queen? That is what I deserve right? So why am I willing to settle down (in the literal and figurative tense) with someone less than that? As every relationship came to an inevitable end for whatever reason, it all boiled down to one constant reason, it may sound cliché but "It's not you, it's me." I realized that it was not the guy's fault, issues or social status, it was all me. I was settling for less than I deserved and desired. I am definitely not one of those women who is willing to settle just to have a piece of a man. No, not me! I can do bad and good by myself. Now don't get me wrong, I do not want to spend the rest of my life alone, however I refuse to spend the rest of my life being super save a ninja and having to dumb down my talents and gifts to make a man feel like a man. Don't get it twisted, I have NO problem being submissive and supporting my man. I just need a man that is doing something I can support.

One day while watching a reality show, I had an epiphany. One of the women on the show was dating a wealthy man and every time she wanted to make an expensive purchase she would simply call him and sweetly ask for what she wanted it could be cars, thousand dollars' worth of jewelry and cosmetic surgeries. He would effortlessly say yes and pick up the check. She would be grateful and move on to the next purchase as if this was normal behavior. As I laid on my couch and processed this, I wondered, "Is it really that easy?" I mean really, how do women find men like that? This woman was white and her boyfriend just said that he wants to make her happy even though she does have expensive taste. Now let that had been a sistah, she would be labeled as a gold digger, prostitute, whore, etc. Why is that? Why is it that white women can allow a man to take complete financial care of them endowing them with lavish gifts and there's nothing wrong with it, but let a sistah do it . . . Is this a double standard? Or is it a matter of African American women being so independent and strong and not willing to allow men to take care of them or having too much pride to ask for what we want? I can only speak from my personal experience. For instance, my relationship with Charles. He was a wealthy man who had the financial ability of buying me whatever I wanted. But for some strange reason I could never bring myself to be that chic to ask for anything. Even when he took it upon himself to buy me things, I was overly grateful and always would try to return the gesture. Why is this? Why do I say I want a wealthy, successful man, but in the same breath not allow him to take care of me and spoil me? A lot of women have this problem. We have been alone, independent and taking pretty good care of ourselves for so long that when we actually have the man we want who is willing and able to take care of us we don't know how to accept the gifts.

Lesson Learned: Women, allow a man to be a man. It's not about owing him something or being accustomed to taking care of men. Figure out what you want and how to ask for it. ASK, BELIEVE, RECEIVE.

NOTES

CHAPTER

WHAT DO I HAVE TO LOSE?

*But seek ye first the kingdom of God, and his
righteousness; and all these things shall be added
unto you.*
Matthew 6:33

Have you ever been in a place where it seems you are the most emotional, hormonal and depressed you have ever been? Feels like you are so full and completely empty all at the same time. I can relate. Every day that passes I am unfulfilled and simply existing. The most pathetic part of it all is that fact that I know how to make things better, but I just cannot seem to bring myself to do what I know is right. God has told me time and time again that if I delight myself in Him and do the things that He has called me to do, then all of my desires will follow. He will open doors of opportunity for me, and I will be elevated and closer to fulfilling my calling. I know that God has an assignment for me to accomplish and some of them are during my time of singleness. If I would just focus, do what He has told me to do, then and only then will He grant me my heart desires which is for my husband to find me and the family I have always dreamed of. So now, tonight as I am writing this I have decided to stop bucking, wasting time and delaying my happily ever. It is time to get to work and busy myself with the work of the Kingdom. I am sick and tired of being sick and tired. It is time for me and you who are reading this to walk in the fullness of God. A life without purpose and active pursuit of it is depressing, boring and pointless (Ask me, I know all too well.).

Lesson Learned:

If you feel unfulfilled, as if your life is just not making sense, remember what God has promised you: That you will live and not die, that you are the head and not the tail, that you are His child, and that He has the last say. *But seek ye first the kingdom of God, and his righteousness; and all these things shall be added unto you. Matthew 6:33*

BETRAYAL

There are so many powerful people in the Bible who were betrayed by someone close to them. For example, Joseph is betrayed by his own brothers. They hated him so much that they conspired to kill him all because of the dreams he had and who he was going to be. It was not Joseph's fault that he was his father's favorite son and that he had a calling on his life to rule over his brothers. Despite his lack of control over who God had called him to be, Joseph is still hated on by his brothers and had to go through a lot before his purpose was fulfilled.

Similar to Joseph, even Jesus was betrayed by someone close to him, Judas. Even though Judas did not conspire to betray Jesus, when the pressure was on he did. When I look at my life and the many, many times that I have been betrayed by the people close to me either family, friends or boyfriends, I can't help but to think of the lives of Joseph and Jesus. These are two men that did no wrong. They didn't ask to be King or the son of God, but they had no control over the plan God had before the earth existed. After being betrayed by people who I thought really loved me, I have come to realize that it is all a part of the process. Going through the process of being hurt, lied to, cheated on, thrown in the pit of life left for dead, placed in jail wrongfully or rightfully and the ultimate sacrifice of giving up our lives for the lives of others is what we as Christians are equipped to do. Is it hard? Yes. Do I want to give up at times? Of course. Do I believe that in the end it will all be worth it? Absolutely. One thing I know for sure is my best day with Christ is still far better than my worse day without Him. For me, that's enough motivation to continue the journey.

Deuteronomy. 29:29 "The secret things belong unto
the Lord our God: but those things which are revealed
belong unto us and to our children for ever, that we
may do all the words of this law."

EVERYTHING HAPPENS FOR A REASON

I believe that nothing happens by coincidence. When bad things happen, people will revert to the cliché "that everything happens for a reason." Yes, that is true, but have you ever taken that a step farther and sought out the reason why it happened? What were you supposed to learn from that bad relationship, failed marriage, miscarriage, abortion, job loss or accident? You can say it happened for a reason, but an even greater thing to know is what God tries to teach us in those situations. There is always a lesson to be learned from the good, bad and even the ugly. Oftentimes, it is hard to see the good in the bad and the lesson in the mess. However, why go through the mess and not get anything from it? I mean, really, if you're going to have to go through the situation anyway, you may as well reap some benefits in the process. I'm not trying to come off as Positive Patti but am just being Realistic Raevyn. As you have read so far, I have been through hell and back in my short years of living. I've experienced extremely high highs and extremely low lows. Would there be some things that I would have done differently? You bet ya. Do I regret anything that I have gone through? Not a one. I may not have dissected my reasoning's for life happenings when I was going through them, but now as I look back over my life and I think things over, I finally realize why God allowed me to go through the things that I did. He wanted to make me stronger, wiser, more persistent, driven, sympathetic, understanding, passionate, loving, kind and so much more. If I had not had father issues, I would not have known that He is my father. If I had not had an abortion, I would have known that God is a God of second, third and fourth chances. If I had not made poor moral decisions and had a criminal record, I would not have seen God be a lawyer in the courtroom, restore my name, and make me a woman of integrity and character. If my life would not have played out the way it did, I would not be writing this book right now and ministering to those who have similar life stores because I would not be able to relate or have anything to talk about. Is my life the perfect, pure sin-less story? Not at all. Am I willing to allow God to get the glory out of my life and bless others? Yes! I did not go through all the hell I went through in vain. This is my story, this is my song, and I will continue to praise my Savior all the day long.

I UNDERSTAND

Sometimes you feel like giving up, and it seems like your best is not good enough. You call unto the Lord and ask Him do you see me? Do you care about all of the things I'm going through?

Sometimes you feel like you are all alone. Feeling like a stranger so far from home. You feel like you have done all you can do and you cry out to the Lord to give you strength and help you make it through. He will respond and tell you to just hold on one more day, take one more step. Don't give up. He knows how much we can bear and when we are in trouble He will always be there. He is preparing you for something great. In those times when you cannot hear His voice, trust His plan because He is the Lord and He understands. He will not change, and He has not forgotten about you. Everything works according to His plan; just trust that He has you in His hands. Always know that God understands.

NOTES

CHAPTER

METHOD TO MY MADNESS

"For my thoughts are not your thoughts, neither are your ways my ways, saith the LORD. 9 For as the heavens are higher than the earth, so are my ways higher than your ways, and my thoughts than your thoughts."

Isaiah 55: 8-9

𝔗here have been times when I think to myself, "Why am I the way that I am? Like really, why do I analyze things the way I do or why do I prefer for things to be a certain way?" The more I ponder my thoughts, God speaks to me clearly. He says, "There's a method to your madness." He led me to *Isaiah 55: 8-9 "For my thoughts are not your thoughts, neither are your ways my ways, saith the LORD. 9 For as the heavens are higher than the earth, so are my ways higher than your ways, and my thoughts than your thoughts."* He confirmed that I am fearfully and wonderfully made. He designed me to be exactly the way I am. He created me to think the way I do, to organize things the way I do all for His purpose to be fulfilled in my life in the Earth. There is a method to what I may think to be madness or weird. His thoughts are not my thoughts; His ways are not my ways. Instead of questioning "Why am I this way?" I ask, "What do you want me to do with the way you have made me?" I truly believe that God has designed me just the way I am and that "thing" that He has made me to do, no one else will be able to do. He did not give them the tools—He gave them to me to get it done.

Lesson Learned: Don't question. Act. There is a method to your madness.

HIGH RISK, HIGH RETURN

Having studied and worked in the financial services industry, I am trained to broker deals involving risk and return. Everyone aims for a high return, however few people want the high risk.

We have all heard the phrase, "Scared money don't make money" in some form or another. In the banking world, that is true. If a client is afraid to invest aggressively, then his return will reflect his fear. I have managed portfolios of all sizes—small businesses with annual revenues of $25 million and middle market commercial clients with annual revenues of $50 million and higher. When speaking with the CEOs and CFOs of these multi-million dollar companies, I always inquire about their business and why they seek to borrow resources. Common responses from presidents or senior vice presidents are we want to grow our business, expansion into new markets, the demand is increasing and we need additional resources to supply our products to the customers. Bank financing is not cheap, though! People like me have to get paid. In the world system, it takes money to make money. These business partners are well aware of that with the high interest rates and loan repayment stipulations. Still, they are willing to take the costly risk to invest in the success of their business.

Being skilled to look at the historical financial statements, calculating cash flow, assessing credit and ratio analysis and researching personal guarantees, I am able to advise the client on the most favorable loan structure for the lender and lendee. As a trusted advisor, my job is to analyze the risk and return for the customer to ensure they understand what the deal entails.

It is inspiring to listen to the founders of these companies selling me their business, sharing their vision, giving the history of how the business started. Their passion resonates in their eyes, body language and voices as they speak on all the company has achieved and the future plans.

How much are you willing to risk? Jesus risked and eventually gave his life for us that we may receive the ultimate return of eternal life. Now that's what I call high risk and high return. Are you willing to risk that one thing you hold on to for a return of even greater value? Those CFOs would risk everything on their businesses because they believe in them that much. God is charging us to risk it all. Not moderately, but aggressively take the risk. We have the best trusted advisor in the business. God. He has structured a deal for you that you cannot pass up. I am a witness: The return is well worth the investment.

YOU CAN'T CONTROL WHAT
YOU CAN'T CONTROL

A close friend of mine was dating this guy who was a NFL player for the Tampa Bay Buccaneers. He was charismatic and treated her with as much respect a young pro athlete would treat girl that is not his wife or really even girlfriend. We would always hang out with the guys and have a good time. They were neighbors and lived right next door to each other. I knew from the beginning that could be really good or really bad. In their case, it was a recipe for disaster. She was physically involved with the guy and really liked him. One day they had an argument and didn't talk for a couple days. Well, one evening she was in her apartment and heard "noises" coming from his apartment. Of course, she placed her ear to the wall connecting her apartment to his to get a closer listen. Do you know this negro was getting it on with another chick right next door! And they had the nerve to be loud! She pulled a Raevyn move and went and knocked on the door. Of course, he didn't come to the door. She was heartbroken and embarrassed. She didn't tell me until days later. I was hurt for her. Only a few days had gone by since their argument, and he was already seeing someone else.

Quick Lesson Learned: Value your self-worth. You are not easily replaceable. What you bring to the table should not be easy to walk away from.

Weeks passed and she avoided him, didn't answer his call or text and she stayed at my house so she wouldn't have to run into him. Eventually, she agreed to speak with him. He tried to act like he missed her and wanted her back. She told him what she heard going on in his apartment that day and that she was hurt. She couldn't believe he would do that to her. He didn't deny what happened and responded by saying "You can't control what you can't control." In that moment, I'm sure that's not what she wanted to hear and so she got mad all over again. When she told me what he said, I agreed with the statement. She had no control over his actions or what he did. It was a hard pill to swallow, but he was going to do what he wanted to do. Period. It was her choice if she wanted to accept that or not. The only control she possessed was over her own actions and what she chose to accept from him.

Lesson Learned: There are many things in life we can control, such as our careers, education, finances and our own actions. The things we cannot control are other people, who we love, or who loves us. A while ago, I diagnosed myself with OCD (obsessive controlling disorder). I realized that I needed to be in control of everything in my life including the people in it. My OCD was exactly what it is called a disorder. It is not realistic or healthy to be controlling. Yes, we all have the capability of controlling what we say, what we do and how we act. However, we cannot control the things that are outside of our control or go out of control when things are not within our control.

The only person who has all control over everything is God. Even God still grants us the right to choose. God is sovereign. All things are under His rule and control. Nothing happens without His direction or permission. *"In whom also we have obtained an inheritance, being predestinated according to the purpose of him who worketh all things after the counsel of his own will:" Ephesians 1:11* The sovereignty of God is not that He has the power and right to govern all things but that He does so, always and without exception. God is not only sovereign in practice but sovereign in principle.

WE ARE WINNERS

I watched a basketball game the other day and it was interesting to see how the game would change as each quarter went by. For the first half of the game the team I rooted for was up by ten points for most of the first half. When the second half began, my team was still going strong and in the lead. In the fourth quarter, the opposing team came back, and soon the game was tied. I was on the edge of my seat due to the intensity of the game. One team would score, then the other team would score, and the clock was ticking down to the last seconds of the game. My team called a time out. I was worried, wondering if they were going to pull it off. I couldn't understand how they would let the other team catch back up after being in the lead for all of the game. The game was neck and neck—tied up. My team had the ball and one last play left before the buzzard would go off. They got back on the court, the clock started and at the buzzard a shot went up in the air. Seemed like it moved in slow motion and as the clock goes off the shot goes in, nothing but net! *Swoosh!* My team won and everyone was happy and celebrating.

The game reminded me a lot about life. As I approach the end of my first quarter of life, I feel like I am up in the game. Yes, there have been some technical fouls, travels, time outs and out of bounds this quarter, but I am still in the game. As life goes on, the game gets closer, more stressful, and tighter all the way to the end. One thing I know for sure is that God is the overall referee of this game called life. He calls the game and has the ultimate say. So, hang in there, play it smart, and know that you are a winner in the end!

NOTES

CHAPTER

15

DISCONTENTMENT

I am not saying this because I am in need, for I have
learned to be content whatever the circumstances.
Philippians 4:11

What's next? Where do I go from here? What else is there in life? What's my next project? What on earth am I here for? These are all questions I have asked myself during each transition in my life. These questions are all rhetorical and repetitive during a time of change.

When I was a child, they did not get asked as much because there is a simple plan laid out: Go to school, get good grades, participate in sports and extracurricular activities year after year until I graduated from high school. That is pretty easy. Once I graduated from high school, the questions began. What college am I going to attend? What major should I choose? How do I survive in the real world without my parents? What do I want to be when I grow up? Next thing I know, college graduation is here. It approached faster than I imagined. I had not really answered all of my questions, however I am now faced with a new set of questions. Who am I? What am I going to do with my life? Do I really like the career that I chose? How am I going to pay all of my bills? As I wandered through life in pursuit of the answers, life continued to move forward. I accomplished milestones and gradually continued each step toward . . . what? Graduated from high school with high honors, check. Graduated from undergrad and graduate school with honors, double check. Blessed with a lucrative corporate America job, check. Now what? Do I continue to live the American dream, climbing up the corporate ladder to the reach the top and find that all this work and time was for nothing? More questions. This seems to always happen to me. I am task/goal oriented. I work toward a goal, achieve it, then become discontent because I do not have anything else to work toward. This cannot be the life that God has for me. Yes, the accomplishments and accolades are great. But these "things" are great on the world's standards. I may be in this world, but not of this world. I want to live unto God's standards. His plan. So the true question is God, what did You create me to do to bring glory to Your name?

Lesson Learned: I truly believe that if we learned what God created us to do, we would never become complacent or discontent. The Bible says in Matthew 6:33, *But seek ye first the kingdom of God, and his righteousness; and all these things shall be added unto you.* When the Bible says "all things," it means just that. All things. How can we become discontent when we are seeking first the kingdom of God (which is a full time job) and in return receiving all things? We cannot. Our lives will be so full of the things of God and in our spare time receiving all the good things of God that we will not have the time to ask why am I here. Instead, we walk in our God-given call and be content living the life that God so graciously and specifically designed for only us.

UNMET EXPECTATIONS

I have found myself time and time again dying with frustration of unmet expectation, dreaming bigger and bigger but not taking the smallest step toward those dreams. Someone once asked me what was my greatest fear in life. My greatest fear is to never fulfill my God given purpose. I fear living a life without purpose. The farther I move away from my purpose, the more a little piece of me dies. Life without purpose is not living, it's merely existing. Going from day to day, month to month and year to year being unfulfilled and ultimately dead. This is not the life God wants His children to have. He has called us to have life and to have it more abundantly. As heirs of the kingdom, we have to take our rightful place. Stop allowing the devil to tell you that you are less than or incapable of being the queen you are. Take your rightful place on the throne! Start your business! Graduate with that degree! Save lost souls! Share your story!

HOPE VS. DESPAIR

Webster dictionary defines hope as "A desire of some good, accompanied with an expectation of obtaining it, or a belief that it is obtainable; an expectation of something which is thought to be desirable; confidence; pleasing expectancy."

There are times when I have found myself extremely hopeful about what the future holds and about life in general. I lived in expectation of great things! Then there are those times when I have found myself in a place of depression, lack of expectancy, and hopeless. I have often wondered how I could feel emotions from both spectrums, sometimes even questioning if I was bipolar. God revealed to me to always look at the opposite emotion. What is the opposite of hope? Despair. Webster's Dictionary defines despair as "To be hopeless; to have no hope; to give up all hope or expectation. God desires for his children to live in hope, love,

134

joy and peace. However, the devil wants us to be the complete opposite. The devil will fight our hope with despair, our love with hate, and our joy with sadness. The enemy's main mission is to kill, steal and destroy. The Lord wants us to live a good life and to live it more abundantly. When the enemy comes against you with despair, pray prayers of hope and quote scriptures like Jeremiah 29:11, *"For I know the thoughts that I think toward you, saith the LORD, thoughts of peace, and not of evil, to give you an expected end."* God's word is your lifeline.

FEELING MEANS DEALING, DEALING MEANS HEALING

I had always suppressed my feelings. I would keep them bottled up inside to one day eventually explode or continue to allow them to eat away at me piece by piece. Both are unhealthy ways to live and over time could be fatal. I needed an outlet, a way to release my frustrations, anger and unfiltered thoughts in a controlled manner. Now, some people choose to discharge their emotions by overeating, alcohol, drugs, sex, and many other self-inflicting ways of pain or numbness to drown their true emotions. I've tried all of those ways and more, and the result remained the same: unsuccessful. When the numbness wears off, the emotions are still there.

The only way to successfully overcome pain is to deal with it. Feel the pain every ounce of it. Deal with it, all of it. Then you are officially ready to heal from it.

NOTES

CHAPTER

16

FREE YOUR MIND AND THE REST WILL FOLLOW

And be not conformed to this world: but be ye
transformed by the renewing of your mind, that ye may
prove what is that good, and acceptable, and perfect,
will of God.
Romans 12:2

$\mathcal{B}$attles of the mind are the hardest to fight. If the devil can get into your mind, he has won half the battle. The mind controls the body. If your mind is sick with stress, low self-esteem, anger, depression, hostility or anxiety, then it is sending all of those symptoms to your physical body. The Bible says, "that as a man thinketh so is he." You have the power to think yourself happy, to think yourself stress free, to think yourself well. There is a literary phrase that promotes education—"the mind is a terrible thing to waste." This statement is so true. If we would recognize the power of the mind and the power it has over our lives, we will have the ammunition to win the battle.

First, we have to guard what we allow to enter our minds wither through movies, music, television shows or what we read. The world system has mastered advertising and creating subliminal messages that subconsciously enter our minds. When I was little, we use to sing a song that said, "I got my feet shod with the preparation of peace, got my sword of the spirit, my shield of faith. Got my breastplate of righteousness, my helmet of salvation. I put on the armor, and I'm ready for the battle." An important part of the armor if the helmet of salvation we have to protect our heads and our minds.

I've heard coaches yell to their players, "Get your head in the game." They know that once the player's head is in the game, their bodies will play accordingly. It all begins with the mind. When I fall into depression or anxiety, my state of being was initiated in my mind then traveled to my heart, emotions and spirit. Once you free your mind, the rest will follow.

"COULDA, WOULDA, SHOULDA"

There are various songs that talk about all that could've been and should've been, if it was not for Jesus. Every time I hear one of those songs, I begin to think back on all the times that I know it could've been me homeless, or in a psychological ward, or broke and not knowing where my next meal would come from. It should've been me in jail, or with a terminal sexually transmitted disease, or dead. It would've been me prostituting my body for money, escaping life's issue with drugs and alcohol, or committing any crime that I thought I was smart enough to get away with. But God! If it was not for the blood of Jesus who kept me and watched over me even when I did not have sense enough to take care of myself . . .

When I look back on the many girls who were pregnant and had abortions and ended up losing their lives because of procedure malfunctions, that could have been me. The times when I was driving on the highway intoxicated and could have killed an innocent driver and myself, that should have been me. The many times I was in places with people that I hardly knew and could have been kidnapped, raped, beat, drugged or murdered, that would have been me. If it was not for an interceding mother, grandparents, aunts, uncles and church family, I could have easily been a statistic. I get emotional when I think back to ALL the stupid stuff I have done and how I could have totally ruined my life for good. But God!

This is why I praise Him and thank Him every day for all of His many blessings. If He does not do one more thing for me, He has truly done enough. I will never be able to repay Him for bringing me out of darkness into His marvelous light. But I will use every day I am given to offer my life as repayment all for His glory.

IT'S NOT ABOUT ME

The more I go through life, the more I realize how much it is not about me! The hurt, pain, lessons learned, and all of the things that I've gone through ultimately is not about Raevyn. It is a difficult concept for our minds to grasp. We go through the hardships of life thinking that these were just the cards I was dealt. I'm just trying to make it through the best I can for me.

These are the lies the devil has programmed our minds to believe. Our lives are predestined and ordered by God. He wants us to use our pain to push through to our purpose. He allowed us to get hurt to help someone through their hurt. There was time when I wanted to give up, throw in the towel, and commit suicide. Life was too hard; I had messed up and did not feel worthy to live. I could not pray because I was too embarrassed to even talk to God. I sinned, went against God and it was all my fault. God stepped in and gave me a glimpse of all of the young girls and women that would give up and die because I chose to be selfish and only think of me when times got hard and unbearable. He showed me the souls that needed to hear my testimony to know that He was real. Yes, I had done wrong, but someone needed to see my wrong in order to make the right decision for their life. I didn't choose to live for me, I chose to live for the lost souls that I was purposed to bring to Christ, the young girls who cries out for a friend, a big sister who has made the same poor decisions she has made to tell her that everything will be okay, that God forgives her and still loves her.

I did not go through all the crap I went through to give up and take my life. Why give up now? Yes, I am bruised and battered. But I am alive. I survived. It the fight didn't kill me, then why would I kill myself? If it didn't kill me . . . it made me want to live for real now! Every situation, setback and disappointment was not purposed for our misery but for our ministry. It's not about you or me. It's about Jesus!

Lesson Learned: There are times when you think you can't pray after *that* mistake. But I learned that it's the only way you can make it better. You're frustrated and feel like you can't take anymore. You ask God when things will get better. Always know that you have someone in your corner, and He will always be there for you. When situations get too much for you to take and you feel like you're going to break, remember that God is there. He will never leave you nor forsake you. Even when you feel like you've gone too far and you've waited too late to pray. God is still there. He loves you, and there's no love greater than His love. Right now, you are hurt and want your pain to end. You probably feel like you can't win, but prayer is the key that unlocks doors. I'm praying for you. Please pray for me. Let's pray for each other. I pray, you pray, we pray!

LETTERS TO MY PAST AND FUTURE

Therefore what God hath joined together, let no man

put asunder.

Mark 10:9

Dear Past,

I am writing this letter to say GOODbye. We experienced some good times and some bad. Finally, I have realized that reminiscing about the poor choices I have made and my experiments gone badly is not worth the regret. I do not regret anything because at one point it was exactly what I wanted. There is no need to cringe when my mind wanders back to the moments when I had no regard for my life or myself, to the many times when I lived life not caring about the consequences and repercussions of my youthful thinking. Fortunately, those moments pushed me to my purpose.

I have become a new creature in Christ. Old things are passed away, and all things have become new. Thank you for all of your lessons. If it were not for you, I would not be the fearless woman I am today. As I look back over the years and all the memories we have shared I am grateful for the times we had together. Even the lowest, darkest and most painful times, I thank you.

I believe that people are in my life for a reason, season or a lifetime. There are a few reasons and seasons that I would like to give my regards. To all of my grueling reasons and wilderness seasons, thank you. I would not have realized I needed help if you would have stayed with me. I would not have realized that you were toxic if you did not force me to leave. You did me a service I would not have done for myself. I am grateful. I refuse to be bitter. I choose to be better. I am certain that God will not waster any of my pain. Thank you for driving me toward my destiny.

Signed,

Moved on

To my Future,

Even though I have not met you, I pray for you. I know you are out there somewhere, possibly hidden and being prepared for me. Please know that I am waiting for you to find me. While I am waiting, God is preparing me to be your wife, your queen. When we meet, be exactly who you are. That's how I will know you, by your spirit.

You are my spiritual soul mate. I know you are already praying for me because I feel your prayers telling me to wait for you. I am praying for you. My prayers are that God will continue to lead and guide you to me, not prematurely but in His time. I promise to no longer give my heart or temple to anyone that is not you. You are worth the wait.

I will know you when I see you. It may not be love at first sight, but there will be an instant spiritual connection. You will check every box on my "new and revised list," you will have the wisdom of Solomon, the leadership of Moses, the faith of Abraham, the fearlessness of Daniel, the forgiveness of Paul, the passion of David, the obedience of Noah, the humility of Joseph and the sacrificial and unconditional love of Christ. You will find me with the courage of Esther, the faithfulness of Ruth, the perseverance of Hannah and the submission of Mary.

I can't wait to be under your covering. Safe and secure in your arms forever. The thought of knowing that I will never have to wonder "is he the one" again is comforting. You are my best friend, my lover and my spiritual guide.

When we meet we will immediately know why it did not work out with everyone else. We will be thankful to the boyfriends/girlfriends that broke our hearts and eventually lead us to each other. I'm waiting on you my love.

Patiently Waiting,
Your Future Wife

BONUS: Love Lessons Learned the Hard Way

- Don't waste your love on the wrong person.
- Patiently wait for God to send the right person for you. Life is too short to spend it with the wrong person.
- You cannot have passion without pain.
- Never confuse what if with what is.
- Sometimes you don't know what you don't know.
- You don't have to look like what you're going through.

NOTES

_____

_____

_____

JOURNAL

What almost killed you?

What lessons have you learned?

What MADE you?

What did it make you? (i.e. stronger, wiser, better)

What's your story?

Why are you still here?

PRAYER

Lord, thank you for not giving up on me and making me better during my time of pain. Thank you for not wasting my pain, but using my sorrow for Your glory. You are so gracious to not allow me to look like what I've been through. Help me to learn the lessons you are teaching me and to use what I've learned to pull someone through their hard times. Continue to make me stronger, wiser, and more anointed in my times of adversity. Please use my mess to enhance my message, my test to intensify my testimony and my pain to find my purpose. Give me the comfort in knowing that regardless what I go through it will not kill me, but make me what You want me to be. Allow me to withstand the pressure and endure the process to become a diamond. Refine me Lord. Purify me so that I can be used by you. I may not be qualified, but I am called. I am willing to die so that Your glory can be shown through me. I am your servant and you are my master. Order my steps in your Word. I did not come this far to turn around. I trust you. I need you. I love you. Amen

ACKNOWLEDGMENTS

When I started writing this memoir over five years ago I was in one of the darkest places of my life. I didn't believe I would ever make it through the pain, hurt, and disappointment. I just knew that my current situations would kill me. There were times I didn't want to live. In the midst of my struggle the Lord allowed me to find comfort in writing; expressing my most personal feelings and emotions on paper. When I didn't have anyone to talk to or was too embarrassed to tell anyone my secrets, I would write them. It was therapeutic for me to journal the occurrences in my life. In the beginning, I never thought I would ever be free enough to share my story to the world, but now I have found freedom in my transparency, healing in my openness and courage in my boldness.

To my Lord and Savior Jesus Christ, thank you for saving me. Thank you for your grace and mercy that has kept me even when I didn't want to be kept. The unconditional love and favor you have shown me can never be matched by an earthly being. You have been my father, boyfriend, husband, attorney, doctor and so much more. All of the times I have messed up and detoured from your will, you forgave me and used my mistakes for your glory. Words cannot express my gratitude. However, I will live every day on this earth to exemplify your love and kindness and do your perfect will.

Mommy, my best friend, my prophetess, my prayer partner, I would not be here today if it wasn't for you (literally). You have trained me up in the way I should go and now that I am older I have not departed from your godly teaching. I cannot imagine loving someone more than I love you. You are my guardian angel. God knew exactly what He was doing when He gave me to you. Thank you for your support, words of wisdom truth and tough love. I am forever grateful for the sacrifices you have made and the phenomenal example you have been to me as a godly woman, wife, mother, daughter, sister and friend. Mommy, it's me and you to the end! I love you 24/7.

To my family and personal "Board of Directors": Granny, Auntie La La, Uncle Tony, Bobby, Jathan, Aunt Ella, Uncle John, Aunt Betty, Mother, Uncle Mark and Aunt Stephanie—thank you for covering me in prayer and interceding on my behalf. Your spiritual and financial support throughout the years has blessed me in more ways than one. I pray that God will allow me to give back to you all a thousand fold. You have always had my back like none other. I have the best family ever! I pray! You pray! We pray!

To my "besties": Nikki and Clarissa—we have been through hell and back together. Thank you for being my ride or die chicks! Nik—We have been best friends for as far as I can remember. We are complete opposites of each other and I think that's why we get along so well. This book told a lot of our secrets that you have kept so well throughout the years. I'm sure we'll have many more to keep. Thank you for always telling me the truth in love. Time to get ready for the sequel! C—When we met in college we had an instant chemistry. I'm convinced you are my alter ego lol. You love hard and are loyal to the core. I never really had many female friends, but you have stood the test of time and drama. I trust you and thank you for always making sure I get a good laugh!

Finally, to all of my friends, supporters, intercessors and church family—THANK YOU! During every chapter of my life you have motivated me to not give up and keep going. You always saw my purpose even when all I saw was pain. I *MADE* it with your help.

Raevyn

Raevyn

Born July 24th on her mother's birthday, Raevyn entered a lineage of greatness. She spent her early years participating in pageants, winning numerous titles including Miss Florida Seafood 2003, Miss Franklin County 2001, Miss Sunburst, and Miss Florida U.S. Continental finalists. Her success in pageantry birthed "Beauty of Holiness," a mother/ daughter ministry created to reach generation to generation through vocal, dance and life teaching.

Born in Orlando, FL, but raised mostly in the rural city of Apalachicola, FL, Raevyn says, she may be a small town girl but has worldwide dreams.

An advocate for education, this scholar graduated from high school with high honors and was early admitted into Florida A&M University, where she graduated cum laude with a Bachelor's of Science Accounting

Degree and her Master's of Business Administration at the age of 21.

Raevyn's unique ability to merge artistic and analytical skills, she has balanced multiple careers ranging from the arts to corporate America, holding fundamental roles with multi-billion dollar companies.

Raevyn has been chosen by God to minister through inspirational speaking, business consulting and development, and mentorship. This multi-talented ambassador for Christ has traveled abroad and throughout the country reaching young adults and youth sharing her life of pain, passion and purpose.

Presently, Raevyn is building a global empire for the Kingdom of God by using her God-given talents of exhortation, the arts and business savvy to help the hurting, to invest in the unprivileged, and to save souls. She has a heart and passion for seeing young people, especially teen girls, grow in the Lord.

150